T0360450

Gender, Embodiment and Fluidity in Organization and Management

This third volume in the *Routledge Focus on Women Writers in Organization Studies* series challenges us to think again about the implications of gender, embodiment and fluidity for organizing and managing. The themes of this book disrupt our understanding of dualisms between sex (men and women), gender (masculinity and femininity) and mind/body, and in so doing analyze the ways in which dominant power relations constitute heteronormativity throughout organizational history, thereby reinforcing mainstream management research and teaching. By centring the work of women writers, this book gives recognition to their thinking and praxis; each writer making political inroads into changing the lived experiences of those who have suffered discrimination, exclusion and marginalization as they consider the ways in which organizational knowledge has tended to privilege rather than problematize masculinity, fixity, control, normativity, violence and discrimination.

The themes and authors (Acker, de Beauvoir, Halberstam, Kosofsky Sedgwick, Kristeva, Yourcenar) covered in this book are important precisely because they are not generally encountered in mainstream writing on management and organization studies. They are significant to the study and analysis of organizations because they demonstrate how our understanding of managing and organizing can be transformed when other voices/bodies/genders write on what it is to work, live, lead and relate to self and others. All the writers turn to the ways in which individuals matter organizationally, acknowledging that lived experiences are a source of political and ethical practice.

Each Woman Writer is introduced and analyzed by experts in organization studies. Further reading and accessible resources are also identified for those interested in knowing more. This book will be relevant to students, researchers and practitioners with an interest in business and management, organizational studies, critical management studies, gender studies and sociology. Like all the books in this series, it will also be of interest to anyone who wants to see, think and act differently.

Robert McMurray is Professor of Work and Organization at The York Management School, UK. Research interests include the organization of health care, professions, emotion labour, dirty work and visual methods. Other collaborative book projects include *The Dark Side of Emotional Labour* (2015), *The Management of Wicked Problems in Health and Social Care* (2018) and *Urban Portraits* (2017).

Alison Pullen is Professor of Management and Organization Studies at Macquarie University, Australia, and Editor-in-Chief of *Gender, Work and Organization*. Alison's research has been concerned with analyzing and intervening in the politics of work as it concerns gender discrimination, identity politics and organizational injustice.

Routledge Focus on Women Writers in Organization Studies

Given that women and men have always engaged in and thought about organizing, why is it that core management texts are dominated by the writing of men? This series redresses the neglect of women in organization thought and practice and highlights their contributions. Through a selection of carefully curated short-form books, it covers major themes such as structure, rationality, managing, leading, culture, power, ethics, diversity and sustainability; and also attends to contemporary debates surrounding performativity, the body, emotion, materiality and post-coloniality. Individually, each book provides stand-alone coverage of a key sub-area within organization studies, with a contextual series introduction written by the editors. Collectively, the titles in the series give a global overview of how women have shaped organizational thought.

Routledge Focus on Women Writers in Organization Studies will be relevant to students and researchers across business and management, organizational studies, critical management studies, gender studies and sociology.
Edited by Robert McMurray and Alison Pullen

Beyond Rationality in Organization and Management
Edited by Robert McMurray and Alison Pullen

Power, Politics and Exclusion in Organization and Management
Edited by Robert McMurray and Alison Pullen

Gender, Embodiment and Fluidity in Organization and Management
Edited by Robert McMurray and Alison Pullen

For more information about this series, please visit: www.routledge.com/ Routledge-Focus-on-Women-Writers-in-Organization-Studies/book-series/ RFWWOS

Gender, Embodiment and Fluidity in Organization and Management

Edited by Robert McMurray and Alison Pullen

LONDON AND NEW YORK

First published 2020
by Routledge
2 Park Square, Milton Park, Abingdon, Oxon OX14 4RN

and by Routledge
52 Vanderbilt Avenue, New York, NY 10017

Routledge is an imprint of the Taylor & Francis Group, an informa business

British Library Cataloguing-in-Publication Data
A catalogue record for this book is available from the British Library

Library of Congress Cataloging-in-Publication Data
Names: McMurray, Robert, 1972– editor. | Linstead, Alison,
    1971– editor.
Title: Gender, embodiment and fluidity in organization and
    management / edited by Robert McMurray and Alison Pullen.
Description: Abingdon, Oxon ; New York, NY : Routledge, 2020. |
    Series: Routledge focus on women writers in organization
    studies | Includes bibliographical references and index.
Identifiers: LCCN 2019035240 (print) | LCCN 2019035241
    (ebook)
Subjects: LCSH: Organizational sociology. | Sex role. | Feminism. |
    Queer theory.
Classification: LCC HM786 .G46 2020 (print) | LCC HM786
    (ebook) | DDC 305.3—dc23
LC record available at https://lccn.loc.gov/2019035240
LC ebook record available at https://lccn.loc.gov/2019035241

ISBN: 978-0-367-23406-5 (hbk)
ISBN: 978-0-429-27970-6 (ebk)

Typeset in Times New Roman
by Apex CoVantage, LLC

Contents

Series note   vi
List of contributors   ix

1   Introduction: Gender, embodiment and fluidity in
    organization and management   1
    ROBERT MCMURRAY AND ALISON PULLEN

2   Joan Acker: Champion of feminist organization theory   8
    YVONNE BENSCHOP

3   When the shoe is on the Other foot: Simone de
    Beauvoir and organization theory   25
    PHILIP HANCOCK AND MELISSA TYLER

4   Julia Kristeva: Speaking of the body to understand the
    language of organizations   42
    MARIANNA FOTAKI

5   Marguerite Yourcenar: Anticipating the (queer) body
    (in organization studies)   59
    CHRIS STEYAERT

6   Witnessing Eve: Eve Kosofsky Sedgwick   75
    SAARA L. TAALAS

7   J. Jack Halberstam   92
    NICK RUMENS

Index   108

Series note

This series arose from the question: given that women and men have always engaged in, and thought, about organizing, why are core management texts dominated by the writing of men? Relatedly, and centrally to the development of organization studies as a field, the following questions become central: Why do so few women theorists and writers appear in our lectures and classes on managing, organizing and working? Why has the contribution of women to organization theory been neglected, indeed, written out of, the everyday conversations of the academy?

This series redresses the neglect of women in organization thought and practice. It does so by highlighting the unique contributions of women in respect to fundamental organizational issues such as structure, rationality, managing, leading, culture, power, ethics, diversity and sustainability, while also attending to more nuanced organizational concerns arising from issues such as performativity, the body, emotion, materiality and post-coloniality.

Through a selection of carefully curated short-form books, the series provides an overview of how women have shaped organizational thought. This series is international in scope, drawing on ideas, concepts, experiences and writing from across Europe, North America and Australasia and spanning more than 150 years. As the series develops our ambition is to move beyond even these confines to encompass the work of women from all parts of the globe.

This is not a standard textbook. It does not offer a chronological history of women in organization theory. It does not (cannot) claim to be the complete or the last word on women in organization: the contribution of women to organization theory and practice continues and grows. We do not even promise that each chapter will be written like the one that preceded it! Why? It is because the variation in style and substance of each chapter deliberately reflects the varied, exciting and often transgressive women discussed. Indeed, one of the points of this series is to draw attention to the possibility that there are as many ways of thinking about, writing on and doing organizing as there are people. If you want to read and think differently about management, work and organization, then this is the series for you.

Readers of this and other volumes in the series will note that the first person is often employed in our accounts of women writers. Reference is made to meetings with writers, to the personal impact of their thinking, and the ways in which writers have moved or challenged their researchers personally. Once again, this personal emotional approach to assessing the work of others is at with odds with more positivistic or masculine approaches that contend that the researcher or analyst of organizations is to remain outside, beyond or above the subject matter: an expert eye whose authorial tone allows them to act as dispassionate judge on the work of others. We argue that the fallacy of neutrality that results from such masculine positivism hides the arbitrary and inherently biased nature of subject selection, appraisal and writing. Just as importantly, it tends to produce sterile prose that does little to convey the excitement and dynamism of the ideas being discussed.

The subject matter of this book has been chosen because the chapter creators believe them to be important, and particular thought has been given to the selection of the women writers shared with you. Authors recognize the bias inherent in any writing project; it is writ large in the title (*Focus on Women Writers*) and is more explicit in some chapters than others. In editing this series, we have been struck with the enthusiasm that informs how our authors have chosen influential women writers, and this enthusiasm can be read in the ways in which the chapters engage with the work of specific writers, the application of these writers to organization studies, and the personal reflections of the influence of writers on their own research. The perspective from which we – and our authors – write is therefore open for you (the reader) to read, acknowledge and account for in the multiple ways intended. The lack of consistency with which the authors address fundamental organizational issues should not be read as lacking rigour but rather bring an alternative way of leveraging critical thinking through an engaged, personal approach to the field. In this way, authors embody the ideas and ethos of the women writers chosen. While written in an accessible form, each chapter is based on years of engagement with the works of particular writers and an in-depth appreciation of their contribution to and impact on organization studies. There is also critique. The omissions or controversies that have accompanied the work of particular writers is addressed, along with challenges to their work.

The result is a collection of books on women writers that are scholarly, readable and engaging. They introduce you to some of the most important concepts in organization studies and from some of the best theorists in the field. Politically and ethically, we hope that this book will help students, lecturers and practitioners reverse a trend that has seen women writers written out of organization theory. Just as importantly, the inclusion of such work usefully challenges many long-held beliefs within mainstream management literature. We hope that this series will be the beginning of your own personal journey of ideas – the text and suggested readings produced in this book offering starting point for your own discoveries.

Routledge Focus on Women Writers in Organization Studies will be relevant to students, teachers and researchers across business and management, organizational studies, critical management studies, gender studies and sociology.

Robert McMurray and Alison Pullen

Contributors

Yvonne Benschop is Professor of Organizational Behavior at the Nijmegen School of Management at Radboud University, the Netherlands. She is Head of the Department of Business Administration and Director of the interdisciplinary research group Gender and Power in Politics and Management. She is interested in the responsibility of organizations for gender equality, diversity and inclusion. She studies the formal and informal processes that produce inequalities in the workplace, and the design, application and evaluation of interventions to change organizations toward equality, diversity and inclusion. Yvonne is Co-editor in Chief of *Organization*, associate editor of *Gender, Work and Organization*, and serves on the editorial boards of several other journals.

Nijmegen School of Management, Radboud University, Netherlands.

y.benschop@fm.ru.nl

Marianna Fotaki is Professor of Business Ethics at University of Warwick Business School, University of Warwick, UK. She holds degrees in medicine and obtained her PhD from the London School of Economics and Political Science. Marianna was Network Fellow (2014–2015) at the Center for Ethics, Harvard University, and co-directed an online think-tank, the Center for Health and the Public Interest (http://chpi.org.uk) pro bono (2014–2017). She has published over 70 articles on gender, inequalities and the marketization of public services appearing in the leading international journals such as *Organization Studies*, *Organization*, *Human Relations*, *Public Administration*, *Sociology of Health and Illness* and *Social Science and Medicine*. Her recent books include *Gender and the Organization, Women at Work in the 21st Century* (Routledge, 2017 co-authored with Nancy Harding), *Diversity, Affect and Embodiment in Organizing* (Palgrave 2019, co-edited with Alison Pullen) and *The Psychosocial and Organization Studies: Affect at Work* (Palgrave, 2014, co-edited with Kate Kenny). Marianna currently works on whistleblowing (funded by the ESRC and British Academy/Leverhulme Trust), solidarity responses to crisis and refugee arrivals in Greece.

Warwick Business School, UK.
marianna.fotaki@wbs.ac.uk

Philip Hancock is Professor of Work and Organization at Essex Business School, University of Essex, UK. His research has been published in a range of academic journals including *Academy of Management Review*, *Organization Studies*, *Human Relations* and *Work Employment and Society*, as well as in co-authored and edited volumes.

Essex Business School, University of Essex, UK.
phancock@essex.ac.uk

Robert McMurray is Professor of Work and Organisation at The York Management School, UK. Research interests include the organization of health care, professions, emotion labour, dirty work and visual methods. Other collaborative book projects include *The Dark Side of Emotional Labour* (Routledge), *The Management of Wicked Problems in Health and Social Care* (Routledge) and *Urban Portraits*.

The York Management School, University of York, UK.
Robert.mcmurray@york.ac.uk

Alison Pullen is Professor of Management and Organization Studies at Macquarie University, Australia and Editor-in-Chief of *Gender, Work and Organization*. Alison's research has been concerned with analyzing and intervening in the politics of work as it concerns gender discrimination, identity politics and organizational injustice.

Department of Management, Macquarie University, Australia.
Alison.Pullen@mq.edu.au

Nick Rumens is Professor in Business and Management at Oxford Brookes University, UK. His main research interests are lesbian, gay, bisexual, transgender and queer (LGBTQ) sexualities and genders in organizations, workplace friendships and queer theory. He has published on these topics in journals including *Human Relations*, *Organization Studies*, *British Journal of Management*, *Organization*, *Journal of Personal and Social Relationships*, *Sociological Review* and *Gender, Work and Organization*. He has also (co)authored and (co)edited books including *Contemporary Perspectives on Ecofeminism* (Routledge, 2016); *Sexual Orientation at Work: International Issues and Perspectives* (Routledge, 2014); and *Queer Company: Friendship in the Work Lives of Gay Men* (Ashgate,

2011). His latest single authored book is *Queer Business: Queering Organisation Sexualities* (Routledge, 2018).
Oxford Brookes Business School, Oxford Brookes University, UK.
nrumens@brookes.ac.uk

Chris Steyaert is Full Professor of Organizational Psychology at the School of Management, University of St. Gallen, Switzerland. He received his Ph.D. in Organizational Psychology from KU Leuven. His current interests concern creativity, multiplicity (diversity) and reflexivity, drawing upon processual, practice-based and queer-theoretical approaches.
School of Management, University of St. Gallen, Switzerland.
chris.steyaert@unisg.ch

Saara L. Taalas is Professor in Business Studies and head of Life at Home and Sustainable Production research initiative at Linnaeus University, Sweden. Her research interests focus on the boundary conditions of management and roles of active audiences in mediated economy. Saara is a human rights activist. Her work has been published in journals such as *Entrepreneurship and Regional Development, Management and Organizational History, Philosophy of Management* and *International Journal of Management Concepts and Philosophy*.
School of Business and Economics, Linnaeus University, Sweden.
Saara.taalas@lnu.se

Melissa Tyler is Professor of Work and Organisation Studies at the University of Essex, UK. Her work on gender, feminist theory and the body; on emotional, aesthetic and sexualized forms of labour; and on work spaces, places and settings has been published in a range of international journals, edited collections and co-authored books. Melissa's recent books include *Soho at Work: Place and Pleasure in Contemporary London* (Cambridge University Press) and *Judith Butler and Organization Theory* (Routledge).
Essex Business School, University of Essex, UK.
mjtyler@essex.ac.uk

1 Introduction

Gender, embodiment and fluidity in organization and management

Robert McMurray and Alison Pullen

Where books 1 and 2 of the *Routledge Focus on Women Writers in Organization Studies* series sought to problematize classic themes of managing and organizing (e.g. rationality, power and politics), the third volume in the series invites the reader to journey through classic, foundational, contemporary and, at times, radical themes surrounding gender, embodiment and fluidity. The writers in this book challenge rigid, simplistic and misplaced assumptions about what it is to manage and be organized. The suggestion that gendered identities are unitary, stable and fixed is questioned. They challenge tacit and explicit presumptions that organizations are either gender neutral or predominantly populated by men and they consider the ways in which organizational knowledge privileges rather than problematizes thought over embodied knowledge, thereby reinforcing the Cartesian divide between mind and body. Work and associated organizational regimes have long been understood to effect people as they discipline, regulation and control individual bodies. Understanding the diversity of bodies, the ways they are regulated and the extent of their agency is important as it raises questions around the ways and extent to which bodies can resist. Whilst the diversity of sexed, raced and classed bodies have been recognized, we need to ask whether the healthy able-bodied have been privileged. This includes disrupting the historically narrow focus of empirical research and organizational writing, where all too often there has been a presumption that working bodies are male bodies or gender-neutral bodies.

Studies of gender difference are well developed in the field of management and organization studies, starting with research that sought to highlight women's different experiences in relation to men. In the field of gender work and organization, the ways in which gender-influenced industrial relations and the fabric of organizational structure, culture and identity has been attended to. Yet despite progress for women, we still witness vast inequalities regarding women's access to equal pay, equality of institutional rights, organizational discrimination and everyday micro-aggressions. There is also much to be done in terms of understanding the ways in which the diversity of identity (and associated intersectional differences) enact inequality in relation to access to paid employment, precarious labour contracts, barriers to organizational progress and violence towards those who depart from the normative basis of the 'ideal worker' who is a white, male, middle-class member of the organization.

Contemporary studies drawing on transdisciplinary scholarship, as testified in this book, further understanding of the ways in which gendered identities and practices, as well as sexuality, are not only multiplicities but also fluid in that we are constantly seeing identity as a performance that is in the process of being done and undone.

The themes of this book disrupt our understanding of dualisms between sex (men and women), gender (masculinity and femininity) and mind/body, and in so doing analyze the ways in which dominant power relations constitute heteronormativity throughout organizational history thereby reinforcing mainstream management research and teaching. By centring the work of women writers, this book gives recognition to their thinking and praxis, each writer making political inroads into changing the lived experiences of those who have suffered discrimination, exclusion and marginalization. All the writers presented employ writing as political practice whether it is through philosophy, craft or film, and these contributions motivate social change and social justice.

Exploring the work of writers such as sociologist Joan Acker, we come to understand how the history of management and organization research has been constructed, and subsequently misread, by masculine rationality that either overlooks or takes little account of gender, of difference or of the power relations that reside therein. Consequently, despite their landmark contributions, 'classic' works such as the Hawthorne studies are myopic and partial. Reading gender into management and organization theory provide more than just an interesting historical footnote or post-hoc corrective. Rather, rewriting organization and management studies to acknowledge its masculine basis warns against the regurgitation of past 'knowledge', lest we reinforce the exclusion, discrimination, violence and mistakes of our past. While this does not call for the erasure of that which has gone before, it does petition for more inclusive re-reading if we are to prevent further sedimentation of outmoded ideas and unwanted biases that continue to violate those who deviate from the norm. This includes rolling back gender-based othering.

Continuing the focus on gender, writers such as Joan Acker, Marguerite Yourcenar and Simone de Beauvoir draw our attention to the ways in which organizational scholarship and practice has positioned women as 'other' who – relegated to the shadows due to the domination of phallocentric discourses – are ignored, marginalized and negated. We come to understand how the divisions wrought by thought and related discourses are social constructions designed to maintain the status quo. Through the work of Julia Kristeva, Jack Haberstam and Eve Sedgwick, the status quo is deconstructed and the permanence, fixity and immutability of identity are cast as political, ethical and aesthetical lived possibilities always in processual becoming. Bodies and their difference are fluid, and it is in this fluidity that marginal identities are freed from the normative ideologies that control them. Thus, static world views and dominant ideologies are disrupted as our writers challenge apparent organizing truths that threaten to forcibly define and constrain to our lives. What is at stake here is not just a reconceptualization of selves but of what it means to live, to organize and to succeed on one's own terms. Taken together, the chapters in this book draw on what are often difficult accounts of marginalization and oppression to construct images of more positive – more human – alternatives to relating to self and other. In this sense, issues of body, gender and fluidity emerge as personal, political and organizational.

We open this third book in the series with a writer who prefigured the very field of gender work and organization: *Joan Acker*. Described by Yvonne Benschop as the scholar who interweaved the worlds of activism, theory and policy, Joan Acker's reach was and continues to be global in scope. Acker's writing and praxis advanced our understanding of hierarchies, power relations, sexism, identity, roles, (un)paid labour, job evaluation, control, neutrality, differential treatment, bodies, classificatory systems and the intersection of sex, class and race. Much of this work drew attention to the ways in which gender relations were implicitly ignored or actively written out organizational practice and management research. Indeed, we come to understand that the Hawthorne Studies would have looked very different if its analysis had included an account of sex, processes of power and control. Yvonne Benschop reminds us that, in the period in which Joan was writing, Acker was among a handful of people opening up these issues as matters of legitimate research and concern. Acker was creating the spaces within which the gendered nature of organized relations could (and should) by examined critically. She challenged society and the academy to confront their regimes of inequality arguing for new theories that would explain how gender, class, race, the body and sexuality are part of the processes of control, differentiation and exploitation in work organizations that are then (re) produced over time and geographies. Revised and revisited, Joan Acker's groundbreaking work has developed the very discourse through which misogyny, inequality and abuse can be resisted, whether in the academy, shop floor, boardroom or Hollywood casting couch.

Philip Hancock and Melissa Tyler present *Simone de Beauvoir* in all of her richness and complexity. Chapter 3 revolves around a key question, namely, how is it that in a collectivity in which we all depend upon each other for mutual recognition of our subjectivity, women are perpetually rendered abject and 'Other'? This is tackled through an account of de Beauvoir's life and writing, paying particular attention to her best-known non-fiction books: *The Second Sex, The Ethics of Ambiguity* and *The Coming of Age*. Through Simone de Beauvoir we come to understand that women are in a relationship that is negated rather than reciprocated, insofar as they are defined in relation to men but neither recognized by men or viewed as that against which men are constituted. As Philip Hancock and Melissa Tyler go on to discuss, de Beauvoir is at pains to demonstrate that this positioning of women is no natural phenomenon – it is not a consequence of birth, but is instead a social, political, cultural and intellectual construct that is to be challenged. As with other writers in this series, de Beauvoir is a transgressive presence insofar as she disrupts social and intellectual norms. Her focus on women, on sex, on relations of power, freedom, embodiment and on writing differently all disrupt the status quo as does the very act/presence of her theorizing. Simone de Beauvoir's account of subjectivity is an embedded, contextually rich account that talks to that which restrains freedom (and recognition) but which is nonetheless based on processual notions of becoming that speak to change, and with it the possibility of reconstructing what it means to be a subject – to be a woman. In concluding, it is noted that the impact of Simone de Beauvoir's work on organization studies is considerable (if often indirect), while its everyday relevance is expertly demonstrated through a case study of PricewaterhouseCoopers and the coercive control of women's bodies and identities at work.

From de Beauvoir we move to Marianna Fotaki's consideration of the much-celebrated work of *Julia Kristeva*. Described as a philosopher, semiotician, literary critic and psychoanalyst, Kristeva's ideas on the body, abjection, language and the other have had a profound influence on feminist thought. As Marianna Fotaki notes, while this work has been underutilized in organization and management studies, it has the potential to reshape how we think about ourselves. We learn that Julia Kristeva's work is deeply processual insofar as it rejects static or essentialist notions of the self, seeing the subject (along with languages and (un)consciousness) as emergent, flowing and always becoming. We come to understand that inherent in this becoming it the process of abjection rooted in the maternal and framed through and by patriarchy that leads to a rejection of the body. The body is rejected because it is associated with the maternal, feminine, impure and subordinate. The idea of abjection is important in organization studies insofar as it has underpinned the theorization of discrimination directed at women in the workplace and across society more broadly. Fotaki goes on to provide examples of the ways in which women are placed in a double bind, whereby they do not wish to collude in the maintenance of dominant patriarchal systems but see little opportunity to do otherwise (where acts of resistance and critique serve to reinforce the marginalized positions of women). As the chapter draws to a close, consideration is given to Kristeva's suggestion that we might be strangers to ourselves. This opens up the possibility that we might all be other (foreigners) in some sense. It is perhaps in recognition of our own otherness – as part of Marianna Fotaki's call for self-reflexivity – that connecting with those people/bodies around and beyond us might be realized. Perhaps then we might reduce the harm we inflict on others.

In Chapter 5, Chris Steyaert invites us to journey into the work and thought of *Marguerite Yourcenar*. The chapter opens with an acknowledgement that Marguerite Yourcenar is, for many, a surprising focus for a series on organization studies. Yourcenar is evoked for her ability to help us think beyond the immediate, obvious and material. Marguerite Yourcenar's particular gift is for encouraging us to think about that which is not said: leaving space for silence and openness. Chris Steyaert suggests that this space is important insofar as it allows us to reflect on that which organization and management studies ignores, marginalizes or rejects. We learn how Marguerite not only wrote about such concerns but also embodied them. As the first woman to be inducted into the French Academy in its 350-year history, Yourcenar worked to point up the failure to recognize the contribution of women, mocked egotistical self-promotion and deconstructed her own being to represent it as toil and process. Marguerite Yourcenar's work is important because it challenges the presumption of a masculine and heteronormative world (that might be said to characterize much management writing) to champion multiplicity, fluidity, queer theory and anti-normative thinking. Marguerite Yourcenar's work is shown to speak to that of Eve Kosofsky Sedgwick (Chapter 6) and to foreshadow Foucault's concern with discipline, ethics and the self, such that it invites a reconsideration of power, politics and ethics in everyday organizing. In short, Marguerite Yourcenar's work requires us to think about the embodied, sensual, queer and challenging in the very widest sense.

Chapter 6 speaks to the life of *Eve Kosofsky Sedgwick* (1950–2009) – literary critic, poet, activist and social theorist, who stories her life through her academic activism, which also removes the boundary between our public and private lives. Her work evokes an embodied account of what it means to exist and make sense of our worlds, as Eve Kosofsky Sedgwick's deconstructs the heteronormativity and performativity that underlie everyday life. Eve Kosofsky Sedgwick is lauded as a key writer in the development of queer theory. Yet despite this contribution, Sedgwick's work has received limited attention in management and organization studies. Saara L. Taalas seeks to challenge this omission by considering the ways in which Eve's writing, craft, storying and activism problematizes the relationship between text and the body. Her multi-layered texts destabilize taken for granted readings of what texts can do. Her embodied writing is political, and when we apply her linguistic writings to management and organization studies we are enriched, but this is not a simple process. Her writing, and Saara L. Taalas's periperformative storying of her own material experiences, show what it is to write marginal, vulnerable and diverse lives that become catalysts for social change. This account queers the relationship between words, bodies and lives to disrupt the normalizing heteronormative arena of the modern business school. As the chapter unfolds, we appreciate the extent to which words come to perform acts that define relationships, particularly when witnessed by an institutional other. When the chapter comes to a close, Taalas alerts us to the ways in which Sedgwick's concern with embodied understanding, relationality and affect suggest a form of knowledge construction that is fluid. This is important insofar as it goes beyond the static revelationary tendencies of much critical management scholarship to opening us up to the possibility of activism beyond the pages of a book. Eve Kosofsky Sedgwick's queer activism reminds us of not only looking forward to imagine new futures, but to learn from the past and the ways history writes itself on the skin. Eve and Saara bear witness to different realities.

In our final chapter, Nick Rumens introduces us to a cultural theorist who challenges the dominance of Western neo-liberal thought and the traditional boundaries that serve to define, limit and constrain us. In bringing *J. Jack Halberstam* to the attention of a wider organization studies audience, Nick Rumens presents a range of texts that outline possibilities for living gender and sexuality differently. We quickly learn that the reach of J. Jack Halberstam's work is significant, spanning as it does film, literature, gender politics, queer theory, anarchy and anti-normativity. Self-identifying as gender ambiguous, J. Jack Halberstam invites us to embrace fluidity and unknowability while at the same time making space for naming selves in relation to others. The main body of the chapter draws our attention to three concepts: female masculinity, failure as queer negativity and gaga feminism. Here Halberstam's work is described as disrupting taken for granted categories and associations – for example the conflation of men and masculinities – so that discourses that shape and bind us may in turn be challenged and reshaped to more positive effect. This includes considering how notions such as success, failure and collaboration might be reconstructed in the light of queer negativity, or how the play of the childish, avant-garde or anarchic embodied in gaga feminism can denote action that is simultaneously disruptive and co-operative. When the chapter draws to a close, attention turns to the research of organization studies scholars whose reading of Halberstam has led them to question what counts as 'leadership' or indeed 'credible' scholarship within a business school. The result is a chapter that offers considerable scope (and hope) to think again about what organizing and living might mean in radically diversifying world.

The themes considered in the above chapters are important precisely because they are not generally encountered in mainstream writing on management and organization studies. They are significant to the study and analysis of organizations because they demonstrate how our understanding of managing and organizing can be transformed when other voices/bodies/genders write on what it is work, live, lead and relate to self and others. All the writers turn to the ways in which individuals matter organizationally, that their lived experiences are a source of political and ethical practice in the ways in which we encounter organizations. This third book in the series therefore puts some of the most interesting and radical theorizing on organizing centre stage.

2　Joan Acker

Champion of feminist organization theory

Yvonne Benschop

American sociologist Joan Acker is amongst the most influential writers in and one of the founders of the field of gender, work and organization. In this collection of women writers in organization studies, she cannot be missed as her thinking about the place and meaning of gender, class and race inequalities in organizations is among the most cited in the field. Joan Elise Robinson Acker (1924–2016) was active as a feminist thinker and writer on issues of gender, class and social inequality in organizations long before there even was a field of gender, work and organization.

She started her academic career with a bachelor's degree from Hunter College, obtained a master's degree from the University of Chicago and received her PhD from the University of Oregon. Working as a sociologist at the University of Oregon from 1967 on, she was one of the founders and the CEO of the Center for the Study of Women in Society at that university in 1973 (Love, 2006), one of the first places dedicated to women studies within the academy. The late 1960s and 1970s were the high times of second-wave feminism, when the women's movement successfully called attention to women's liberation, violence against women, the body, reproductive rights and labour market inequalities. Joan Acker was a pioneer in bringing the topics from the women's movement within the walls of the university. By translating activism into research, she built knowledge about women's working lives and with that knowledge laid the groundwork for the development of academic strands of feminism. She used the feminist research findings to advocate policy changes within and outside the university, translating research back to activism again. One example is her participation in the Oregon State Task Force for Comparable Worth, in which she fought for raising the wages of women working low-wage jobs in the state system (Love, 2006). While many academic centres of women and feminist studies that emerged in the 1960s, '70s and '80s disappeared again over the past decades, the Center for the Study of Women in Society is still funding feminist scholarship at the University of Oregon today.

A short biography of Joan Acker is included in the book *Feminists Who Changed America 1963–1975* (Love, 2006). Striking as that may be, Joan Acker's work did not only change America: it had a truly international reach and appeal. The 2012 special issue of *Equality, Diversity and Inclusion* on Joan Acker's contributions to theorizing gender and organization, and the 2018 Joan Acker Gedenkschrift Special Issue in *Gender, Work and Organization* (https://onlinelibrary.wiley.com/journal/14680432) are but a few examples of this international reach. Acker has conducted empirical research both in the United States and in Europe, more in particular during research visits to Sweden and Germany (Acker, 1991b; Acker, 1994), and has always kept up with theoretical developments on both sides of the Atlantic. Joan Acker was a laurelled scholar in sociology who received several prestigious awards for her work, such as the Jessie Barnard Award for feminist scholarship (1989) and the American Sociological Association W.E.B. DuBois Career of Distinguished Scholarship (1993) (American Sociological Association, www.asanet.org).

Acker's landmark publications, both books and journal articles, cover as much as five decades. This long track record is even more impressive because Joan Acker kept rethinking and renewing her theories and regularly published new reflections on the development of the field. By revisiting her own interpretations, adding new contexts and incorporating new insights, she guided the development of the field of gender, work and organizations to the mature state it is in today. In this chapter, I will discuss her main contributions chronologically and thematically, starting with her early work on the sex structuring of organizations, going from comparable worth and job evaluation systems to the theory of gender in organizations including the body and sexuality at work and ending with inequality regimes and intersectionality. I will locate the different contributions in the temporal and contextual developments of the time they were developed.

Breaking ground for the sex structuring of organizations and society

Acker's first publications date from the early 1970s and they revisit key concepts and theories from sociology and organization studies from the perspective of women, demonstrating how power processes result in sexism and organizational hierarchies that favour men over women. In the time and context of the early 1970s, feminist scholarship was being invented by women like Joan Acker, who started carving out places to ask research questions about the positions of women in society, something they had to do in universities largely dominated by men and male perspectives. These first publications have set the stage for a stream of critical feminist re-readings of the assumptions and conclusions of mainstream theories and concepts, and for the articulation of a whole new series of research questions examining the impact of sex in organizations and society at large. The intertwinement of sex and power emerges as a read thread through Acker's writings. In her article in the *American Journal of Sociology*, Acker takes issue with social stratification studies (Acker, 1973). Social stratification, the classification of people in different strata or classes of power, status, occupation and income, is a key theme in sociology. She notes how they have typically overlooked the female half of humanity in their study of social structures, even when sex is one of the most obvious bases of economic, political and social inequalities (p. 936). Her analysis shows how defining women's positions and status as derived only from their family roles and the positions of their husbands obscures sex-based inequalities in stratification systems. Her 'seeing women as persons in their own right, rather than as appendages to men' (p. 941) is a strong feminist plea for the acknowledgement of the intellectual sexism in the study of stratification systems and a recognition that power structures and power relations produce sex-based inequalities in social structures. This early work contains both a critique of the status quo in scholarly stratification studies that does not consider sex-based inequalities and articulates an alternative highlighting the status and position of women making them a 'legitimate problem for the sociologist' (p. 944). Acker has put sex inequality on the agenda of social stratification studies. Her intervention has been successful as illustrated by the many studies following her example. In 1980, she was therefore able to publish a paper in *Contemporary Sociology* in which she reviewed the emerging literature that separates class stratification from sex stratification. She concluded with the assertion that a new stratification theory is necessary; a theory 'that includes women will have to conceptually bridge the gap between women's unpaid and paid labour and bring the structural sources of sex inequality into the analysis' (Acker, 1980, p. 33).

In a similar vein, Acker collaborated with Donald van Houten to examine the sex structuring of organizations in their classic 1974 article in *Administrative Science Quarterly*. Sex structuring is defined as 'the differentiation between female and male jobs, a hierarchical ordering of those jobs so that males are higher than females and are not expected to take orders from females' (Acker and Van Houten, 1974) ((1974) 1992, p. 16). This paper constitutes one of the first feminist analyses within management and organization studies. It re-analyzes the famous Hawthorne Studies on the effects of supervision and autonomy on workers' productivity and Michel Crozier's work on bureaucratic control in French bureaucracies from a sex power perspective. They show that in both studies a considerable occupational segregation by sex exists that is ignored in the original studies, but their re-analysis shows that the sex structuring of organizations has profound impact on the findings of both studies. Acker and van Houten uncover sex differences in socialization, the selective recruitment of compliant women in jobs requiring dependence and passivity, and organizational control mechanisms in line with patriarchal control in society (p. 27). They document how women workers are controlled more strictly than their male colleagues. The authors develop a sophisticated research agenda looking into the relations between sex, processes of power and control and organizations, needed to come to a better and more comprehensive understanding of organizational phenomena.

Acker's pioneering work has been followed by other analyses of management and organization theories from feminist perspectives (e.g. Ferguson, 1994 on bureaucracy and Phillips and Taylor, 1980 on skill). She was among the first scholars to explicate that traditional theories incorporate white men only, and that these theories cannot easily be fixed by 'adding women and stir'. We see here a first appeal for the development of new theories that take into account the lived realities of women in society and organizations, a theme that will reoccur throughout Acker's writings.

Money, money, money: job evaluation and comparable worth

A second important theme in the work of Joan Acker concerns wage as 'an essential component of the capitalist economic system' (Acker, 1988, p. 480). Acker studies waged and unwaged labour as classification and compensation systems from the 1980s onwards. By then, the concept of gender had replaced the notion of sex as the core analytical category (Scott, 1986), making way for sophisticated feminist analyses of the social construction of gender. In Acker's work, it is never only about gender, as the relation between gender and class is a leading thread throughout her work. This is why Marta Calás and Linda Smircich (Calás and Smircich, 1996; 2006) position Acker among the socialist feminists in their famous overview of feminist approaches to organization studies. Acker is influenced by feminist critiques of Marxism articulated in dual systems theory, with capitalism and patriarchy as analytical distinct systems of classed and gendered power relations that meet and interact to produce gendered divisions of labour and gender inequalities in the workplace (Hartmann, 1979). Yet Acker wants to delve deeper in the central theory of bureaucratic or organizational structure to critically question the assumption that organizations are gender-neutral (Acker, 1988).

Inspired by the women's movement, Acker takes up the politically charged and sensitive topic of wage setting, aiming to analyze wages and the wage gap between men and women as a gendered and classed phenomenon. The ideal of a family wage for men, the gendered division of labour with women in particular types of sectors, occupations and jobs and men in others, and the hierarchical order of work organizations with more women in the lower and more men in the higher echelons all amount to persistent wage differences between the sexes (Acker, 1988). In the 1980s comparable worth, or equal pay for work of equal value, is seen as an important strategy to change wage disparities and achieve greater sex equity in wages. Comparing women's jobs with men's, Acker studies job evaluation systems and comparable worth strategies in a number of empirical contexts from the Oregon State Task Force on Compensation and Classification Equity to Swedish banks. This research had been published in a number of reports, book chapters, journal articles and her book *Doing Comparable Worth* (Acker, 1991a).

Job evaluation takes a central role in wage setting as 'the process of assessing the worth of particular job categories on a number of dimensions or compensable factors usually including knowledge and skill, effort, responsibility and working conditions' (Acker, 1987, p. 183). Typically portrayed as technical, value-free and gender-neutral systems, Acker uses feminist research to demonstrate how job evaluation systems are power-laden instead, with male employers and managers holding the bulk of definition power. In one paper (1987), she provides an in-depth account of the negotiations over the modification of the reputed job evaluation system of Hay to make it bias-free and correct inequities between female- and male-dominated jobs. Her analysis shows that compensable aspects of women's jobs can be neglected, that there are links between skills and masculinity, thus demonstrating the gendered construction of job evaluation and how job evaluation is a key process in the reproduction of gender and class hierarchies. In another paper (Acker, 1991b), she delves into the black box of wage decisions to understand how wage setting practices in Swedish banks become gender based. This happens through an accumulation of many small decisions on individual cases that are singled out as special but always pertain to white men. It also happens through assumptions of men as career oriented, and through the undervaluation of women's accomplishments and commitment, especially for women who work part-time or take care leave. Furthermore, patterns of sex segregation allow the assessment of women and men without comparing them, 'maintaining the argument that they do different work that should be valued differently' (1991b, p. 403).

It is clear that the empirical job evaluation and comparable worth projects have sparked and fuelled Acker's interests to develop a comprehensive feminist theory of gender in organizations, or as Adkins phrases it, a materialist feminist sociology (Adkins, 2018). Her analyses of comparable worth projects provided her not only with an opportunity to think critically about wages as a material and crucial part of capitalist production systems, but also helped her theorize how organizations are structured through the intertwining of gender and class inequalities. This means that in organizations, class relations are always gendered and gender is constructed through class. The theoretical implications of this stream of research are further elaborated in her later work that often contains references to job evaluation systems. There are also profound practical implications as these early analyses of the wage gap point to issues that remain relevant for pressing remuneration questions today: the power to individualize wages systematically privileges white men at the top of organizational hierarchies.

The first feminist theory of gendered organizations

This brings us to the part of Acker's work for which she is arguably most famous: the theory of gendered organizations. She is the first author to explicitly articulate a systematic feminist theory of gender in organizations. This theory is laid out in two highly cited publications: 'Hierarchies, Jobs and Bodies: A Theory of Gendered Organizations', published in *Gender & Society* (1990) and 'Gendering Organization Theory', published as a book chapter in *Gendering Organizational Analysis* (Mills and Tancred, 1992). These were written in the context of the late 1980s and early '90s, when the women's movement had gained ground in the universities and managed to cultivate several strands of academic feminism in many different disciplines. This resulted in a wealth of knowledge about gender in society and in organizations from different philosophical and political feminist perspectives (Calás and Smircich, 1996). Yet Acker notes how the managerially inspired questions of organizational efficiency that dominate management and organization theories spark little interest from feminists (Acker, 1990). The influence of feminists on traditional management and organization theories thus remains limited, as persistent assumptions of objectivity and gender neutrality prevail in this domain that systematically ignores gender, women and sexuality. Acker's goal is to bring together the new knowledge on women at work in a systematic feminist theory of organizations that is able to explain the dynamics of gender in organizations. With 'women in management' as the dominant framing of the research problem at the time within management and organization studies, Acker shows here that the gendered division of labour entails much more than the representation, behaviour and leadership styles of women in management jobs. She argues that a new theory is needed to explain how gender, the body and sexuality are part of the processes of control in work organizations, how organizational processes create gendered divisions of labour and gender inequalities in income and status, and to understand the role organizations play in the (re)production of cultural images of gender and gender identities (1990).

A final reason for a feminist theory of organizations is the 'feminist project of making large-scale organizations more democratic and supportive of humane goals' (1990, p. 140).

A strong point in Acker's work throughout the years is her ability to come up with definitions of complex notions such as the 'gendered organization'. To say that an organization is gendered

> means that advantage and disadvantage, exploitation and control, action and emotion, meaning and identity, are patterned through and in terms of a distinction between male and female, masculine and feminine. Gender [and race, class, sexuality, age, ability] is an integral part of those processes, which cannot be properly understood without an analysis of gender.
>
> (Acker, 1990, p. 146)

This idea opened up many opportunities to better understand the complexity and the embeddedness of gender in organizations for different audiences. There is a close connection between Acker's theory of gendered organizations and conceptual developments in gender studies in the late 1980s. There, several authors presented layered notions of gender going beyond dichotomous notions of men and women and distinguishing symbolic, structural and identity dimensions of gender (Harding, 1986; Scott, 1988). Acker was the first to translate these dimensions of gender to the realm of work and organizations.

The heart of the theory of gendered organizations is formed by a set of underlying and interacting processes that reproduce gendered organizations. These different gendered processes are analytically distinct, but part of the same reality. They connect organization level processes to human actions. Even while the theory centres on gendered processes, in Acker's work it is never just about gender inequalities but always about gender in relation to class and race inequalities, although this is more explicit in the 1990 article than in the 1992 chapter.

The first set of processes is the production of gender divisions, for instance in jobs, tasks, skills, wages or hierarchies. The gendered division of labour, gendered divisions of locations in physical space, and gendered divisions of power become manifest in many patterns and varieties, but men are almost always dominant and women subordinate in the hierarchies. This first set is also referred to as the structure processes; the processes that pertain to organization structuring in the composition of jobs, the coordination of tasks and work processes and the allocation of personnel over jobs and tasks (Benschop and Doorewaard, 1998a). The second set are the cultural processes: the construction of symbols, images, metaphors that create, confirm or challenge gender divisions. For Acker, organizations are a core site for the production of cultural norms and values about gender through gender images that always contain implications of sexuality and infuse organizational structures (Acker, 1992, p. 253). An example of such a cultural process is the use of the image of the strong, successful business leader – an image saturated with masculinity. The third set of processes are the social interactions between women and men, women and women, men and men. These interactions are part of the daily work in organizations, whether they are between supervisor and subordinate, workers and customers, or organizational insiders and outsiders. People do gender in these interactions, for instance by sharing or withholding information, interrupting each other, and ascribing status in different ways. The fourth set of processes is concerned with the construction of gendered identities in organizations. Individual people are identified – and they identify themselves – as men and women, 'constructing their understanding of the organization's gendered structure of work and opportunity and the demands for gender-appropriate behaviours and attitudes' (Acker, 1992, p. 253). Gendered self-presentations at work happen through appropriate language, dress and behaviour.

In the 1990 article, there is a fifth set of processes that does not reappear as such in the 1992 chapter. This fifth set concerns how gender is a constitutive part of larger social structures, such as families, kinship and also organizations. This fifth set is called the organizational logic. Organizational logic in traditional and mainstream organization studies is typically seen as gender neutral, but Acker draws on the work of Dorothy Smith (1987) to argue how a gender substructure underlies abstract organizational theories and is reproduced in daily work rules, activities and routines (1990, p. 147). The gendered substructure is mentioned in the 1992 chapter as underlying the gendered processes and defined as 'the spatial and temporal arrangements of work, in the rules prescribing workplace behavior and in the relations linking workplaces to living places' (1992, p. 255). Dye and Mills (2012) call attention to the disappearance of the fifth gendering process and make a plea for a refocus on the fifth process of the organizational logic to analyze the dynamic ways in which organizations are gendered, how they become gendered and how gendered processes change over time. In her review of this article by Dye and Mills, Acker (2012) explains the disappearance of the fifth process of organizational logic by her difficulty at the time to conceptualize the differences between 'organizational logic' and 'organizational substructure', making the first obsolete in comparison to the gendered substructure. It characterizes Acker's propensity to rethink her earlier work that she agrees with Dye to keep organizational logic in the centre of the theory of gendered organizations. It also points to the difficulties to work with this analytical framework as precise distinctions between the different sets of gendered processes are often difficult to make (Benschop and Doorewaard, 1998a; Dye and Mills, 2012). Acker summarizes it as follows:

> the gendered substructure of organizations consists of processes and practices of organizing that continually recreate gender inequalities. These processes and practices are supported by organizational cultures and reproduced in interactions on the job, shaped in part by the gendered self-images of participants.
>
> (2012, p. 219)

The theory of gendered organizations is the place for Acker to further articulate her ideas about the body in organizations. Building on her earlier writings about the stricter control of women's bodies in comparison to men's bodies at work (1974), she unpacks here how the body and sexuality are objects of and resources for managerial control. Featuring prominently in the title of "Hierarchies, Jobs, Bodies" (1990), the attention for bodies helps Acker to analyze the categories of hierarchies and jobs as abstractions, to be filled with evenly abstract workers. Building on the feminist standpoint theory of Dorothy Smith (990) and on Carol Pateman's (Pateman and Grosz, 1986) critique of the politics of liberal individualism, her analysis of this abstract worker sheds light on what the underlying idealizations of workers mean for organization theory. By examining the rules and codes that prescribe workplace behaviour and the crucial hierarchical relation between work and private life, it becomes clear that these rules and claims are based on the abstraction of the disembodied worker, an 'ideal' neutral worker who has no body, no feelings and no gender (Acker, 1992, p. 425). The characteristics of the ideal worker are geared to the organizational context only, and any obligation or disruption from outside the work environment is organized out. Job evaluation is a clear case in point here, as job evaluation is an institutionalized way of making only the job count differentiating between levels of skill, complexity and responsibility, but not between the people who hold it (1990, p. 149). The ideal worker for this abstract job thus becomes an abstraction too, portrayed as a universal individual who can be full time available, highly qualified, mobile, and can be only oriented to work. These ideal characteristics are presented in organizational texts and theories as abstract and neutral, and this obscures that they fit the day-to-day reality of men workers much better than those of women workers, for whom the public and the private sphere are not separate domains (Benschop and Doorewaard, 1998b). So by calling attention to the absence of the body within organization theories, Acker is able to show one of the key principles of gendered organizing through the notion of the ideal worker. In her own, often cited words, 'the concept of the universal worker excludes and marginalizes women who cannot, almost by definition, achieve the qualities of a real worker because to do so is to become like a man' (1990, p. 150).

In the wake of the absence of the body come the absence of sexuality, emotionality and procreation in organizational theory, so that organization processes become separated and sanitized from processes that require bodies. Acker draws on the emerging research on sexuality in organizations (Hearn and Parkin, 1987) to show how gendered processes necessarily include manifestations of sexuality. Sexual harassment is an obvious example, but also the way gendered hierarchies are maintained by the sexualization of women's bodies at work, a phenomenon found typically in women's jobs that centre around serving men, as in the case of flight attendants or secretaries (MacKinnon, 1979; Pringle, 1988). The sexualization of women also occurs in male-dominated jobs such as top management or skilled technical work, in which women are excluded to avoid 'potentially disruptive sexual liaisons' (Lorber 1984, in Acker, 1990, p. 152). Men's bodies are also sexualized, but in different ways with positive connotations of valuable organizational resources and as a way to legitimize the power of men leaders, representing them as strong, attractive and successful (Calás and Smircich, 1991).

The feminist theory of gendered organizations is Acker's strongest contribution – the jewel in the crown of her oeuvre, as Adkins (2018) puts it – and the one that in retrospect has been constitutive of the field of gender, work and organization. As the first author to provide the field with a theory of its own, she provided a major impetus to the development of two formerly separate areas (gender and organization) in one mature field of study. Her theory has since been used widely as an analytical framework to understand the gendered substructure of organizations. It has been expanded, complicated, refined and used in different empirical settings. Other notions, such as gender subtext (Benschop and Doorewaard, 1998a, 1998b; Bendl, 2008), gender logic (Kelan, 2010) or gender regime (Acker, 1994; Walby, 2004; Connell, 2006) have been used. The ideal worker has been differentiated to account for different ideals in different organizational and occupational contexts, showing how a dominant masculinized ideal worker norm appears in many professional settings (Tienari, Quack, and Theobald, 2002; Kelly et al., 2010). Of course, the feminist theory of organizations has also been the subject of critique. Acker herself revisited her earlier notion of the gendered substructure to avoid an essentialist and ahistorical argument, emphasizing the privileging of organizations in capitalist society and the successful organizational claims for non-responsibility for human reproduction and survival (1998b, p. 198). More recently, some authors argue that the feminist theory of gendered organizations has become dated after more than 25 years and that it is unsuited to capture the complex dynamics of the new economy (Williams, Muller, and Kilanski, 2012) or the political economy in which control by finance capital trumped organizational control (Adkins, 2018). Yet, I am unconvinced that the framework of the structural, cultural, inter-relational and identity constructing processes is necessarily tied to the power relations and organizational realities of the time of development. The overall framework can still be an inspiration to understand the gender practices of and in contemporary organizations and processes of organizing (Benschop and Van den Brink, 2018).

Doing justice to intersectionality: inequality regimes

Acker may have gained the most fame for her feminist theory of organizations, but the final contribution I want to discuss here is more exemplary of her scholarship over the five decades. This final contribution is the notion of inequality regime, defined as 'loosely interrelated practices, processes, actions, and meanings that result in and maintain class, gender, and racial inequalities in particular organizations' (Acker, 2006), 443). From 2000 on, Acker's writings become more and more explicitly focused on the inter-relations between class, gender and race and she starts to develop her ideas about inequality regimes. Key publications dealing with this issue are her article in *Social Politics* titled 'Revisiting Class: Thinking from Gender, Race, and Organizations' (Acker, 2000), the article in *Gender and Society* on 'Inequality Regimes: Gender, Class and Race in Organizations' (2006), and her book *Class Questions: Feminist Answers* (also 2006). It should be noted that while the category of age is largely absent in Acker's work, she has made an impact with age as well. There are few scholars who can be applauded for publishing a very influential book in their eighties (Benschop and Van den Brink, 2018).

She develops these ideas in a time (early 2000s) in which feminist theories of organization expand rapidly in different directions, from liberal, radical, psychoanalytical and socialist feminisms to social constructionist, poststructuralist, post-colonial and transnational feminisms (Benschop and Verloo, 2016; Calás and Smircich, 1996; 2006). The most popular strand is liberal feminism as indicated by research on the low representation of women in management and positions of leadership, gendered career patterns and the possibilities or impossibilities of work-life balance. Under the influence of a political-economic climate of increasing neoliberalism and free market capitalism, business case arguments celebrating the contribution of gender and diversity to organizational performance and the bottom line gain popularity in the field of gender, work and organization. In that light, Acker's attention for multiple inequalities goes against the zeitgeist, as it is more in line with critical socialist feminist theorizing that would only gain currency again after the 2008 financial crisis.

Acker draws on her work from the 1970s on class and gender to bring together theories of patriarchy and capitalism and more recent insights that theorize the intersectionality of class, gender and race. She combines the classic system focus of socialist feminist theory with the newer recognition of the importance of intersectional inequalities to build a conceptual framework for the analysis of inequality regimes in organizations. Acker argues that organizations are a key site for the production of inequalities, that these inequalities are always gendered, classed and racialized simultaneously, and that we need to come to a better understanding of the complex, mutually reinforcing or possibly contradicting ways that these inequalities intersect within organizations. Intersectional analyses have been advocated by feminists of colour for 30 years (Crenshaw, 1997) but have hardly been taken up in management and organization studies. With the demand to focus on intersectionality, Acker is once again at the forefront of organization studies by providing guidance as to how to research these complex intersectionalities in organizations and everyday working life.

The conceptual framework of inequality regimes starts with a definition of inequalities as

> the systematic disparities between participants in power and control over goals, resources, and outcomes; workplace decisions, such as how to organize work; opportunities for promotion and interesting work; security in employment and benefits; pay and other monetary rewards; respect; and pleasures in work and work relations.
>
> (2006, p. 443)

It goes on to identify the key components of inequality regimes, emphasizing how these processes and patterns vary in different organizations. First, class, gender and race are explained as the key bases for inequality in organizations. Second, the organizing processes of inequality regimes are identified, in particular organizing work into jobs and hierarchies, recruitment and hiring, wage setting and supervisory practices and informal interactions at work. These are the processes that are used to achieve organizational goals and characterize daily organizational life, but these are also the processes that produce and maintain classed, gendered and racialized inequalities. Third, Acker notes how the visibility (the degree of awareness about inequalities), and the legitimacy (the degree to which inequalities are regarded rightful) of inequalities vary across organizations and across different inequalities. Not all inequalities are visible as inequalities; for instance men tend not to see gender privileges, and whites tend not to see race privileges (Acker, 2006). Hierarchical differences between managers and subordinates are usually invisible as class inequalities, the wage differences between managers and subordinates are seen as legitimate, and many gender and race inequalities are legitimized by arguments of meritocracy ('we want the best, gender nor race matters, only quality does'). High visibility and low legitimacy of inequalities may help to stimulate changes in the inequality regime. Fourth, inequality regimes are maintained through organizational controls and compliance. Acker explains how inequality regimes draw on different types of control, such as direct control through bureaucratic rules, rewards or coercion; indirect control through monitoring technologies, restricting information, or restricted employment opportunities, and internalized control through beliefs in the inevitability of inequalities and the legitimacy of privilege (2006, p. 454). All components are illustrated with examples of how class, gender and race inequalities intersect in different, complex ways. The persistence of intersectional inequalities in organizations does not leave much hope for the possibilities of changing the inequality regimes. Acker, however, firmly states that inequality regimes can be challenged and changed, although she readily acknowledges that this is no easy task. Her recipe for change encompasses a limited change effort, geared towards a specific inequality producing practice. Furthermore, the involvement of the state and social movement actors alongside organizational insiders characterizes successful changes, as does coercion or threat of loss (2006, p. 455).

Elsewhere, I regretted how the systematic analysis of the interrelated sets of processes from the early '90s was replaced by more concrete organizing processes in the framework for inequality regimes (Benschop and Doorewaard, 2012). Acker responded that we need both abstract concepts of the locations of inequality processes and an analysis of concrete practices to 'flesh out abstract structures as well as cultural, interrelational and identity constructing processes' (Acker, 2012b, p. 209). Re-examining her own ideas, as we have seen her do several times, Acker also makes some amendments to her ideas about intersectionality in inequality regimes. Acknowledging the complexity of analyzing inequality regimes, she emphasizes focused research questions that explicitly take into account the intersections of class, gender and race, and qualitative research methodologies to increase the chance that the least visible or obvious and the most deeply embedded manifestations of class, gender and race inequality can emerge.

Conclusion

Joan Acker's work is of vital importance to organization studies and it changed the way we think about organizations, making abundantly clear how organizations function as producers of multiple inequalities based on the intersections of class, gender and race. Her five decades of scholarly and activist accomplishments are a formidable legacy for many in the field of gender, work and organization to fall back on, draw inspiration from and cite in respect. Whether it is her critical rethinking of classic organization theories from the perspective of gender, her materialist analyses of wage setting and comparable worth, or her feminist theories of gendered organizations and inequality regimes, all her writings breathe a feminist stance fuelled by a fascination for power dynamics at work. Upon her passing in 2016, many people wrote that her unapologetically feminist scholarship was a source of encouragement for them. Her many accomplishments show how that research can be meaningful beyond the ivory tower of the academy, and can be used to demonstrate the responsibilities of organizations to change inequality regimes.

Recommended reading

Original text by Joan Acker

Acker, J. (2006). *Class questions, feminist answers*. Lanham, MD: Rowman & Littlefield.

Key academic text

Special issue on Joan Acker's theorizing in *Equality, Diversity and Inclusion*, 2012, ed., S. Sayce, 31(3).

Accessible resource

Special Issue celebrating the work of Joan Acker in *Gender, Work and Organization*, 2018. Available at https://onlinelibrary.wiley.com/toc/14680432/0/0

References

Acker, J. (1973). Women and social stratification: A case of intellectual sexism. *American Journal of Sociology*, 78, pp. 936–945.

Acker and Van Houten (1974). In *Administrative Science Quarterly*; this reference is included and was reprinted in Mills, A. and Tancred, P. (eds.) (1992). *Gendering Organizational Analysis*. Newbury Park: Sage.

Acker, J. (1987). Sex Bias in Job Evaluation: a Comparable Worth Issue is book chapter 9. In: Bose, C. and Spitze, E. (eds.) *Ingredients for women's employment policy.* New York: State University of New York Press.

Acker, J. (1988). Class, gender, and the relations of distribution. *Signs: Journal of Women in Culture and Society,* 13, pp. 473–497.

Acker, J. (1990). Hierarchies, jobs, bodies: A theory of gendered organizations. *Gender and Society,* 4, pp. 139–158.

Acker, J. (1991a) *Doing comparable worth.* Philadelphia, PA: Temple University Press.

Acker, J. (1991b) Thinking about wages: The gendered wage gap in Swedish banks. *Gender & Society,* 5, pp. 390–407.

Acker, J. (1992). Gendering organizational theory. In: A. J. Mills, and P. Tancred, eds., *Gendering organizational analysis.* Newbury Park: Sage, pp. 248–260.

Acker, J. (1994). The gender regime of Swedish banks. *Scandinavian Journal of Management,* 10, pp. 117–130.

Acker, J. (1998). The future of 'gender and organizations': connections and boundaries. *Gender, Work & Organization,* 5(4), 195–206.

Acker, J. (2000). Revisiting class: Thinking from gender, race, and organizations. *Social Politics: International Studies in Gender, State & Society,* 7, pp. 192–214.

Acker, J. (2006). Inequality regimes: Gender, class, and race in organizations. *Gender & Society,* 20, pp. 441–464.

Acker, J. (2012a). Gendered organizations and intersectionality: Problems and possibilities. *Equality, Diversity and Inclusion: An International Journal,* 31, pp. 214–224.

Acker, J. (2012b). Joan Acker's review of the contributing papers, edited by Susan Sayce. *Equality, Diversity and Inclusion: An International Journal,* 31, pp. 208–213.

Acker, J. and Van Houten, D. R. (1974). Differential recruitment and control: The sex structuring of organizations. *Administrative Science Quarterly,* pp. 152–163.

Acker, J. R. (1980). Women and stratification: A review of recent literature. *Contemporary Sociology,* 9, pp. 25–35.

Adkins, L. (2018). Work in the shadow of finance: Rethinking Joan Acker's materialist feminist sociology. *Gender, Work & Organization.* https://doi.org/10.1111/gwao.12227

Bendl, R. (2008). Gender subtexts – Reproduction of exclusion in organizational discourse*. *British Journal of Management,* 19, pp. S50–S64.

Benschop, Y. and Doorewaard, H. (1998a). Covered by equality: The gender subtext of organizations. *Organization Studies,* 19, pp. 787–805.

Benschop, Y. and Doorewaard, H. (1998b). Six of one and half a dozen of the other: The gender subtext of Taylorism and team-based work. *Gender, Work & Organization,* 5, pp. 5–18.

Benschop, Y. and Doorewaard, H. (2012). Gender subtext revisited. *Equality, Diversity and Inclusion: An International Journal,* 31, pp. 225–235.

Benschop, Y. and Van den Brink, M. (2018). The godmother of gendered organizations: In celebration of the work of Joan Acker. *Gender, Work & Organization.* https://doi.org/10.1111/gwao.12231

Benschop, Y. and Verloo, M. (2016). Feminist organization theories: Islands of treasure? In: R. Mir, H. Wilmott, and M. Greenwood, eds., *The Routledge companion to philosophy in organization studies.* London and New York, NY: Routledge, pp. 100–112.

Calás, M. B. and Smircich, L. (1991). Voicing seduction to silence leadership. *Organization Studies,* 12, pp. 567–601.

Calás, M. B. and Smircich, L. (1996). From 'The Woman's Point of View': Feminist approaches to organization studies. In: S. Clegg, C. Hardy, and W. Nord, eds., *Handbook of organization studies.* London: Sage, pp. 218–257.

Calás, M. B. and Smircich, L. (2006). From the 'Woman's Point of View' ten years later: Towards a feminist organization studies. In: S. Clegg, C. Hardy, and T. Lawrence, et al., eds., *The Sage handbook of organization studies.* London: Sage, pp. 284–346.

Connell, R. (2006). The experience of gender change in public sector organizations. *Gender Work and Organization,* 13, pp. 435–452.

Crenshaw, K. (1997). Intersectionality and identity politics: Learning from violence against women of colour. In: M. L. Shanley, and U. Narayan, eds., *Reconstructing political theory.* Oxford: Polity Press.

Dye, K. and Mills, A. J. (2012). Pleading the fifth: Re-focusing Acker's gendered substructure through the lens of organizational logic. *Equality, Diversity and Inclusion: An International Journal,* 31, pp. 278–297.

Ferguson, K. E. (1994). On bringing more theory, more voices and more politics to the study of organization. *Organization,* 1, pp. 81–99.

Harding, S. (1986). *The science question in feminism.* Milton Keynes: Open University Press.

Hartmann, H. I. (1979). The unhappy marriage of Marxism and feminism: Towards a more progressive union. *Capital & Class,* 3, pp. 1–33.

Hearn, J. and Parkin, W. (1987). *Sex at work: The power and paradox of organisation sexuality.* Basingstoke: Macmillan; New York: St Martin's Press.

Kelan, E. K. (2010). Gender logic and (un) doing gender at work. *Gender, Work & Organization,* 17, pp. 174–194.

Kelly, E. L., Ammons, S. K., Chermack, K., et al. (2010). Gendered challenge, gendered response: Confronting the ideal worker norm in a white-collar organization. *Gender & Society,* 24, pp. 281–303.

Love, B. (2006). *Feminists who changed America 1963–1975.* Urbana: University of Illinois Press.

MacKinnon, C. A. (1979). *Sexual harassment of working women: A case of sex discrimination.* New Haven, CT: Yale University Press.

Mills, A. and Tancred, P. (eds.) (1992). *Gendering Organizational Analysis.* Newbury Park: Sage.

Pateman, C. and Grosz, E. (1986). *Feminist challenges: Social and political theory.* Winchester, MA: Allen & Unwin.

Phillips, A. and Taylor, B. (1980). Sex and skill: Notes towards a feminist economics. *Feminist Review*, 6, pp. 79–88.

Pringle, R. (1988). *Secretaries talk: Sexuality, power and work*. Sydney: Allen & Unwin.

Scott, J. W. (1986). Gender: A useful category of historical analysis. *The American Historical Review*, 91, pp. 1053–1075.

Scott, J. W. (1988). Deconstructing equality-versus-difference – Or, the uses of post-structuralist theory for feminism. *Feminist Studies*, 14, pp. 33–50.

Smith, D. E. (1987). *The everyday world as problematic: A sociology for women*. Boston: Northeastern University Press.

Smith, D. E. (1990). *The conceptual practices of power: A feminist sociology of knowledge*. Toronto: University of Toronto Press.

Tienari, J., Quack, S. and Theobald, H. (2002). Organizational reforms, 'ideal workers' and gender orders: A cross-societal comparison. *Organization Studies*, 23, pp. 249–279.

Walby, S. (2004). The European Union and gender equality: Emergent varieties of gender regime. *Social Politics: International Studies in Gender, State & Society*, 11, pp. 4–29.

Williams, C. L., Muller, C. and Kilanski, K. (2012). Gendered organizations in the new economy. *Gender & Society*, 26, pp. 549–573.

3 When the shoe is on the Other foot

Simone de Beauvoir and organization theory

Philip Hancock and Melissa Tyler

Simone de Beauvoir is arguably one of the twentieth century's most significant contributors to feminist theory and politics. This chapter considers the continuing importance of her writing for organization studies, examining major themes and the enduring significance and contribution of her thinking to understanding the persistence of gender inequality in contemporary organizational life.

The chapter begins with a discussion of de Beauvoir's biography, reflecting on the circumstances in which she wrote. As Judi Marshall (2000, p. 167) has commented, alluding to both de Beauvoir's intellectual project and some of the more problematic aspects of her thinking, her articulations are very much 'of their time and context'. Like many other feminist writers, de Beauvoir's work deliberately blurred boundaries between theory, literature and autobiography, weaving together the philosophical, political and personal.[1] Throughout the vast corpus of her fictional and non-fictional writing she developed an explicitly feminist commitment to the phenomenological view that we engage with the world and others as situated, embodied beings, simultaneously the subjects and objects of our existence. As well as her own life, de Beauvoir's writing also needs to be considered through her connections with other philosophers in order to fully appreciate the development and impact of her work both at the time it was written and subsequently. In the opening section and throughout the chapter, we tease out Hegelian influences in de Beauvoir's writing, focusing on her critique of the gendered organization of the desire for recognition as a recurring theme in her work, and considering the relevance of this to contemporary feminist approaches to organization studies.

We then introduce recurring themes in her best-known non-fiction books, primarily *The Second Sex, The Ethics of Ambiguity* and *The Coming of Age*. At the risk of over-simplification, tying together these complex works is a concern to understand how, in a collectivity in which we all depend upon each other for mutual recognition of our subjectivity, women are perpetually rendered abject, and hence become 'Other'. A specifically feminist reading drives de Beauvoir's critique of this 'tragic ambiguity' as she describes it (de Beauvoir, 1976 [1948], p. 7). Notable contributions to work and organization studies that have drawn on de Beauvoir's writing, and insights such as these will then be considered. The continuing empirical and theoretical relevance of her work will be emphasized throughout the chapter, but particularly so in the final section. Here we examine how de Beauvoir's situated understanding of women's embodied experience and subjection to a process of Othering provides the foundation for a critical feminist analysis of gender not simply within organizational life, but as a process of organization in itself (Tyler, 2014). This argument is developed with reference to an incident in which PricewaterhouseCoopers (PwC), based in the City of London, sent a woman home for not wearing high-heeled shoes to work. The series of events that followed this action are considered through the lens of de Beauvoir's writing on gender, embodiment and ethics.

Inevitably, in a chapter of this nature and length, it would be impossible to do justice to either the breadth or complexity of de Beauvoir's writing,[2] to the depth of the texts considered here or to the full details of the PwC case. Our aim, therefore, is to introduce the ideas as best we can, and to make connections that we hope might be taken further; with this in mind, we end with suggestions for further reading.

De Beauvoir's life and work

De Beauvoir was born on 9 January 1908 in Paris, where she lived for most of her life until she died aged 78, and where she is buried next to Sartre in the Cimitière du Montparnasse. Her bourgeois upbringing involved a convent education, and in her autobiographical works she recalls how she was deeply religious until a crisis of faith in her teens meant that she remained an atheist for the rest of her life. An ardent traveller and public intellectual, de Beauvoir worked prolifically as a writer, correspondent, editor, political activist and teacher, with many of her closest 'disciples' becoming close friends and shared lovers of hers and Sartre's. Aside from her own work, de Beauvoir is well known for her lifelong relationship with Sartre, whom she (famously) met whilst preparing for the highly competitive agrégation at the École Normale at the age of 21. De Beauvoir was the youngest person ever to pass the exam, and she was placed narrowly second to Sartre, an experience that arguably shaped the intellectual bond between them that lasted for the rest of their lives.

In addition to Sartre, de Beauvoir's intellectual circle included Merleau Ponty and Camus. The philosophical legacy of Hegel and Leibniz also heavily influenced her work, and she grounded her thesis at the Sorbonne in the work of the latter. From Leibniz, de Beauvoir derived her interests in process and perception; from Hegel, her commitment to exploring the human need for recognition and reciprocity. Other major influences on her thinking included Husserl and Heidegger. De Beauvoir drew heavily, and developmentally, on Husserl's writing on intentionality, and from Heidegger she developed a hermeneutic way of understanding our relationship to the social world and others. The phenomenological existentialism de Beauvoir derived from these various influences fed her enduring preoccupation with the conditions of human freedom and the consequences of its disavowal. This preoccupation was not simply a philosophical one for de Beauvoir, who remained dedicated to integrating her personal, intellectual and political activities throughout her life. This commitment was reflected in the role that she played in the formation of several important political groups and journals, and in her activist contributions.

Along with Merleau Ponty, Sartre and de Beauvoir set up the political journal *Les Temps Modernes* at the end of World War II. She remained an editor until her death, and it was here that she published early instalments of *The Second Sex* and *The Ethics of Ambiguity*. In her later years, she became involved in a series of feminist political campaigns, most famously signing the Manifesto of the 343 in 1971, a list of well-known women who claimed to have had an abortion (illegal at the time in France, but legalized in 1974 largely as a result of the impact of the Manifesto and the feminist movement more widely).

De Beauvoir's writing included novels, essays, biographical and autographical works, and monographs on politics, philosophy and ethics, much of it combining different forms and genres, perhaps most obviously *She Came to Stay* (de Beauvoir, 1984), a melancholy reflection on the relationships between several characters in hers and Sartre's intimate circle. A similar fusion of genres can be found in *Adieux* (de Beauvoir, 1985), her 'Farewell to Sartre', in which she offers a painful and personal account of her last years with Sartre, noting at the beginning that it is the only published writing of hers that Sartre had not read. Her best-known work, *The Second Sex*, arguably included all of these elements in the form of a detailed analysis of women's oppression that seamlessly blends philosophy, history, social commentary, literary analysis and autobiography. As Rowbotham (2009, p. ix) writes in her foreword to the 2009 translation, 'In *The Second Sex* Beauvoir is at once a thinker, a scholar and a creative writer'.

Becoming woman as Other: Themes in de Beauvoir's major non-fiction works

The Second Sex sold 22,000 copies during its first week of publication, and it has since become a classic feminist text. Heavily influenced by Hegel's

philosophy of inter-subjectivity, narrated through his 'master-slave dialec-
tic', the processual ontology underpinning the book provides the philosophical premise for its central preoccupation with the gendered organization of
the desire for recognition. The text's primary concern lies in understanding
the ways in which gender is driven by our ontological need for recognition
within social relations of mutual reciprocity. This underlying conviction
leads de Beauvoir into a distinctly feminist account of the Hegelian dia-
lectic, situating recognition within structural relations of gender inequality
and oppression. This enables her to develop a critique of both the negat-
ing effects of the gendered conditions of recognition, and of the consequences of women's perpetual mis-recognition, or negation. It is the latter,
she argues, that results in women's relegation to a secondary status. As she
puts it, 'the relation of the two sexes is not that of two electrical poles: the
man represents both the positive and the neutral. . . . Woman is the negative, Without Reciprocity' (de Beauvoir, 2011, p. 5, emphasis added). Here,
de Beauvoir maps out the basic premise of her account, namely that what
it means to be a woman is to be a human being driven by but at the same
time denied recognition, 'without reciprocity'. Hence, 'she determines and
differentiates herself in relation to man, and he does not in relation to her;
she is the inessential in front of the essential. He is the Subject; he is the
Absolute. She is the Other' (de Beauvoir, 2011, p. 6).

Analytically, de Beauvoir's (2011, p. 7) interest is in understanding how
and why women's Otherness or non-reciprocity comes about: 'How is it . . .
that between the sexes this reciprocity has not been put forward, that one
of the terms has been asserted as the only essential one, denying . . . its
correlative, defining the latter as pure alterity?' For de Beauvoir, women
are ascribed the status of the Other not as a result of their inherent biology
or psychology, or even because of their material circumstances, but as the
outcome of an ontological process through which one becomes the Other as
the consequence of a series of social constraints and compulsions attached
to the gendered organization of the desire for recognition. In other words,
women become Other because they feel compelled to assume a subjectivity that they feel will be recognized as suitably or appropriately 'feminine'.
This latter theme she explores in more depth in *The Coming of Age* through
a critique of the ways in which older people are 'othered', a point to which
we return below.

With no self-conscious feminist movement in France at the time (Duchen,
1986), and with its explicit references to female sexuality, *The Second Sex*
was both radical and shocking (Marshall, 2000) when it was first published.
Writing explicitly about women's sexuality within a heavily male-dominated
intellectual milieu, de Beauvoir was not only politically bold but philosophically so; 'most disturbing to the defenders of the status quo was the mix

of sex and philosophy. A woman theorizing in sensuous language broke all the rules of containment' (Rowbotham, 2009, p. xi).[3] Even though aspects of de Beauvoir's writing now appear misguided or simply dated, *The Second Sex* continues to be a highly influential feminist reference point particularly given the book's central concern with the question of 'why woman has been defined as Other' (de Beauvoir, 2011, p. 17).

Widely regarded as the intellectual starting point for second-wave feminist theory, one of the book's most enduring preoccupations is with understanding the process through which society comes to be organized so that one becomes the Other. In what is perhaps the most oft-quoted line from *The Second Sex*, de Beauvoir sums up, simultaneously, the book's central concern and thesis, namely that 'One is not born but rather, becomes woman' (de Beauvoir, 2011, p. 293). Becoming a man or a woman is articulated here as a dynamic social process, one that acknowledges both the capacity of social construction and the weight of compulsion (to 'become' in a particular way). It is precisely this dynamic inter-relationship between agentive capacity, social compulsion and structural constraint that de Beauvoir encapsulates in this widely quoted line, and which characterizes the processual ontology underpinning *The Second Sex* (and many of her other works), and arguably feminist theory subsequently. As Kruks has put it:

> In her account of women as subjects 'in situation', *de Beauvoir can both acknowledge the weight of social construction*, including gender, in the formation of the self and *yet refuse to reduce the self to an 'effect'*. She can grant a degree of autonomy to the self – as is necessary in order to sustain key notions of political action, responsibility, and the oppression of the self – *while also acknowledging the real constraints on autonomous subjectivity produced by oppressive situations*.
> (Kruks, 1992, p. 92, emphasis added)

Here de Beauvoir approaches subjectivity in way that is neither removed from, nor caught up in, biological, material or discursive determinism, but instead positions the self as 'in situation', simultaneously socially compelled and constrained (see also Kruks, 2001; 2012). As Kruks notes (see also Calás and Smircich, 2000), de Beauvoir eschews here both a liberal, rationalist take on the subject and a poststructuralist view, framing this distinction as a manifestation of unrecognized human ambiguity (de Beauvoir, 2000).

In her first major non-fiction work published in 1948, *The Ethics of Ambiguity* (2000), de Beauvoir draws heavily on Hegel's (1979 [1807]) inter-subjective ethics and connects to Merleau Ponty's (2002 [1948]) post-dualist ontology of the subject. She does so in order to emphasize that what it means to be human is inherently ambiguous. This is because we are simultaneously (ostensibly) free subjects and, at the same time, 'factic' objects.[4] As free beings (subjects) we have the capacity to make choices and exercise judgement, and as 'factic' (objects) we are constrained by physical, social and political limitations and are subject to the will of others. Without recognition of this ambiguity, ethical conduct is simply not possible, as we perpetually risk treating each other only as objects to whom we are averse. This aversion leads to the Other's objectification, as those we encounter come to be regarded as unworthy of or incapable of providing recognition, rather than (mutually) recognized as subjects upon whom we are inter-dependent. This mis-recognition of each other, and of our mutual inter-dependency, is the dominant theme of *The Coming of Age* (de Beauvoir, 1996 [1972], p. 2), and the philosophical basis of its political (and autobiographical) critique of how society comes to treat older people 'as outcasts'. Connecting this critique to her earlier analysis of women's position as Other in *The Second Sex* leads de Beauvoir to emphasize that within the context of her situated embodiment, woman is condemned to perpetual immanence, unable to achieve the self-consciousness necessary for emancipation ('transcendence' in existential terms). For her, this is because women cannot recognize their own subjugation, internalizing their secondary status instead.

In its simplest form, her thesis in *The Second Sex* is therefore a critique of the conditions of recognition, and of the consequences of mis-recognition, for it is not merely woman's Otherness but her subjection – the nonreciprocal objectification of what it means to be a woman – that de Beauvoir is concerned with. For her, it is this nonreciprocal objectification – the social situation, or organization – of the desire for recognition that precludes relations of reciprocity between the sexes:

> Hence woman makes no claims for herself as subject because she lacks the concrete means, because she senses the necessary link connecting her to man without positing its reciprocity, and because she often derives satisfaction from her role as *Other*.
> (de Beauvoir, 2011, p. 10, original emphasis)

What de Beauvoir calls 'the drama of woman' (Ibid., p. 29) – what it means to become a woman – lies in the fundamental conflict between the existential aspirations of every subject ('freedom') and the compulsions of a concrete or 'situated' existence in which femininity is equated with Otherness. This creates a vicious circle for women so that

> in all analogous circumstances: when an individual or a group of individuals is kept in a situation of inferiority, the fact is that he or they are

inferior. But the scope of the verb *to be* must be understood; bad faith means giving it a substantive value, when in fact it has the sense of the Hegelian dynamic: to *be* is to have become, to have been made as one manifests oneself.

(Ibid., p. 13, original emphasis)

Here de Beauvoir notes that if a woman is oppressed to the point whereby her subjectivity is denied her, then her situation is *de facto* her 'destiny' and comes to be perceived as such. However, what de Beauvoir derives from Hegelian philosophy is the conviction that the gendered self is not a static state of being, but rather a constant process of becoming. As she (Ibid.: 46, original emphasis) puts it (drawing again on Merleau-Ponty), 'woman is not a fixed reality, but a becoming, she has to be compared with man in her becoming; that is, her *possibilities* have to be defined'. The search for an underlying essence of womanhood is therefore futile and misguided; for her, men and women are ultimately the same in their potential ('possibilities') as human beings, but this 'sameness' is distorted through the social location of woman as the (ontologically inferior) Other – through her relegation to the 'second sex', or what de Beauvoir describes as 'her concrete situation' (Ibid.: 15). For de Beauvoir, women cannot enter into the struggle for recognition in Hegelian terms because they cannot recognize themselves as oppressed: 'woman's drama lies in this conflict between the fundamental claim of every subject, which always posits itself as essential, *and the demands of a situation that constitutes her as inessential*' (Ibid.: 17, emphasis added).

Developing an existentialist conception of the human condition as a project of becoming into something more discernibly feminist, she maintained that women are compelled to conform to a feminine (passive, inferior) role in order to 'be', to be accepted as feminine, and so sustain the very relations of difference that constitute the foundation of their oppression. That is, they are required to 'become' in ways that ultimately serve to sustain their oppression simply in order to be recognized as feminine; a recognition that is, however, conditional, and which traps women (in existentialist terms) in a perpetual state of immanence. As she poignantly put it, 'her wings are cut and then she is blamed for not knowing how to fly' (de Beauvoir, 2011, p. 660). What is significant about this is that women not only accept their entrapment but perpetually, and painfully, aspire to it as a sign of femininity. The ensuing embodied servitude that women don't simply live and experience but positively embrace as a sign of viable femininity, de Beauvoir describes as 'a state of serfdom':

It follows that woman knows and chooses herself not as she exists for herself but as man defines her. She has to be described first as men dream of her since her *being-for-men is one of the essential factors of her concrete condition.*

(de Beauvoir, 2011, p. 159, emphasis added)

In the last third of *The Second Sex* (in what for many are its most problematic sections – see Evans, 1996), de Beauvoir outlines three strategies women might pursue. First, women must support themselves financially (striving for economic autonomy) through paid work: 'when she is productive and active, she regains her transcendence' (de Beauvoir, 2011, p. 737). It is important to note, however, that de Beauvoir also cautions that a woman who works unpaid in the home and on a paid (but exploited) basis within the labour market carries a 'double servitude' (Ibid.: 739); not only are working women independent only within the confines of an oppressed class, their paid work outside of the home does not free them from unpaid work within it, and persistent patterns of labour market segmentation mean that even within paid work, most women 'do not escape the traditional feminine world' (Ibid.: 738). Hence,

> The woman embarks on a career in the context of a highly problematic situation, subjugated still by the burdens traditionally implied by her femininity.
>
> (Ibid.: 753)

Second, women should strive to become intellectuals – a theme that has been developed by proponents of '*l'ecriture feminine*', such as Hélène Cixous (1986), who urge women to 're-inscribe' themselves into the political process through their writing (see Höpfl, 2011). This, in de Beauvoir's view, helps to address the fundamentally epistemological problem of women's Otherness; in her words, to unravel the extent to which 'representation of the world, as the world itself, is the work of men; they describe it from a point of view that is their own and that they confound with the absolute truth' (de Beauvoir, 2011, p. 166).

The final, and most important strategy for women to take part in is political transformation through social reorganization, and de Beauvoir urges women to act as agents of social change. She did not put her faith entirely in the development of a post-capitalist utopia, however, acknowledging that there will always be some differences between men and women. These, she argued in particularly problematic passages of *The Second Sex*, are primarily corporeal – relating to men and women's different ways of 'being' in the body. Drawing directly on Merleau Ponty's (2002, p. 409) post-Cartesian understanding of embodiment, developed most fully in his *Phenomenology of Perception*, de Beauvoir understands embodiment as the process through which lived materiality and subjective consciousness merge or 'intertwine': 'I am thus my body in as much as I have experience, and reciprocally, my body is like a natural subject' (Merleau Ponty, 2002, p. 232, cited in de Beauvoir, 2011, p. 42). Put simply, for de Beauvoir, 'the body is not a thing, *it is a situation*: it is our grasp on the world and the outline for our projects' (Ibid.: 46, emphasis added).

De Beauvoir's descriptions of women's relationship to their bodies are somewhat ambivalent, constituting on the one hand, a shameful burden, and on the other, a source of wonder, to be adorned and displayed:

> It is a burden: weakened by the species, bleeding every month, passively propagating, for her it is not the pure instrument of her grasp on the world but rather an opaque presence; it is not certain that it will give her pleasure and it creates pains that tear her apart; it contains 'threats': she feels danger in her insides. . . . Her body escapes her, it betrays her; it is her most intimate reality, but it is a shameful reality that she keeps hidden. And yet it is her marvellous double; she contemplates it in the mirror with amazement; it is the promise of happiness, a work of art, a living statue; she shapes it, adorns it, displays it.
>
> (de Beauvoir, 2011, p. 672)

Further to the criticisms to which *The Second Sex* has been subject for its portrayal of women's bodies, de Beauvoir has also been criticized for her acceptance – even celebration – of male ideals (see Kruks, 1992; Moi, 1994). Indeed, in some sections of the text she appeals directly to a predominantly male notion of abstract, universal freedom as the goal for the truly liberated woman, urging women to 'overcome' their burdensome bodies and embrace male rationality. Noted by many critics has been the way in which the last word of *The Second Sex*, literally, is granted to a call for an unequivocal affirmation of fraternity.

In sum, *The Second Sex* has been

> called racist as it did not account for Black women's experience; heterosexist or homophobic for its depiction of lesbian women as sexually abnormal; patriarchal for accepting male terms of reference and lacking in any notion of woman centred-ness; [and] exclusive because of its existentialist framework and difficult language.
>
> (Duchen, 1986, p. 166)

These criticisms notwithstanding, few feminists (even those who number its most vehement critics) would deny that *The Second Sex* has been a major influence on contemporary feminism. Toril Moi (1994, p. vii) has perhaps put it most passionately, arguing that

> *The Second Sex* is both a major philosophical text and the deepest and most original work of feminist thought to have been produced in [the twentieth] century. . . . Feminist thought can benefit immensely from serious reconsideration of *The Second Sex*, not as a historical document illustrating a long past moment in feminist thought, but as a source of new philosophical insights.

Noting the need to remind ourselves that, as Marshall (2000) has put it, *The Second Sex* was very much of its time and context, it is to the book's continuing capacity to provide philosophical insight that we now turn, focusing specifically on the development of this capacity within organization studies.

De Beauvoir and organization studies

Whilst de Beauvoir's writing has been the subject of sustained engagement within feminist theory, with a few notable exceptions, organizational scholars have tended to draw more indirectly on her work, commonly citing contemporary theorists who themselves have been influenced by de Beauvoir (Hancock and Tyler, 2007; Phillips and Knowles, 2012; Pullen and Knights, 2007). This means that the impact of the latter's writing can be felt quite widely, if not directly or obviously, across the field. Judith Butler (1990), whose work has been increasingly influential, acknowledges the debt she owes to de Beauvoir, tracing her own preoccupation with the conditions of recognition and the consequences of mis-recognition, back to de Beauvoir's dual concern with gender as a productive social process and with the social conditions compelling and constraining that process.

De Beauvoir's influence within organization studies can be discerned in two broad ways. First, in studies acknowledging and advancing an ontological shift in the way in which gender is understood, emphasizing gender as a social or discursive practice characterized by fluidity, multiplicity and performativity (Czarniawska, 2006; Jeanes, 2007; Kerfoot and Knights, 1998; Martin, 2003; 2006; Pullen, 2006; Pullen and Simpson, 2009). In this body of work, the enduring and widespread influence of de Beauvoir's processual ontology can be discerned, traceable through West and Zimmerman's (1987) formative paper on 'doing gender' and Butler's (2004; 2005) more recent writing on gender as a perpetual process of 'un/doing'. What this body of work derives from de Beauvoir is both a vocabulary for analyzing 'becoming' gendered, or rather assuming a social position as a gendered subject, as the outcome of a (perpetual) process of social construction – of compulsion and constraint, and a basis for developing a critique of this process.

Second, a rich body of research has evolved, much of which draws from this processual ontology, that has highlighted women's positioning as Other within and through organizational life. Otherness is a concept that is introduced early in *The Second Sex, The Coming of Age* and *The Ethics of Ambiguity* and which arguably connects the feminist critique developed in all three texts. While the focus of these three books is (respectively) on women's otherness as gendered, aging, objectified subjects, de Beauvoir (1978, p. 144) emphasizes that 'the Other is multiple' and the concept has become central to feminist analyses of the intersectional forms assumed by oppression. In an incisive call for listening as a form of political praxis, Swan (2017), for instance, emphasizes the multiple ways in which indigenous peoples become 'doubly' Othered through unreflexive accounts of their historical exploitation and through contemporary re-appropriations of their experiences. Similarly, Ahmed (2006, p. 79) paraphrases de Beauvoir's critique of women's Otherness asking what it might mean to posit straightness as a becoming if 'One is not born, but rather becomes straight' (see also Ahmed, 2017).

Notable examples of work within organization studies that draws directly on de Beauvoir's critique of women's Otherness include Phillips and Knowles's (2012) discussion of the performativity of women business owners which shows how 'women's entrepreneurship is Othered' within popular cultural discourses. Gherardi (1996), Kerfoot and Knights (2004), and Simpson (2011) also cite de Beauvoir in their respective discussions of the ways in which organizational processes assign an inferior status to femininity, as does Jeanes (2007) in her critique of gender binaries that construct woman as the Other as an obstacle to organizational equality. Bolton (2005) also cites de Beauvoir in her discussion of the ceremonial work undertaken by women working as gynaecology nurses as they challenge their relegation to a secondary status; re-framing themselves as Other in a way that collectively embraces the marginal status attributed to their work and skill as a position of strength and solidarity. Powell, Bagilhole, and Dainty (2009, p. 414) also explore the ways in which women engineers do and undo gender with reference to de Beauvoir's discussion of how 'woman is socially constructed as the Other'. Similarly, Mavin and Grandy (2016, p. 1098 and 1095) draw on de Beauvoir in their study of the 'abject appearance' of women elite leaders' embodied identities. Their concern is to illustrate and understand how women leaders 'manage' the ambiguities of their abject status, occupying formal positions of power, and thereby ostensibly achieving 'parity with the One' yet at the same time, remaining marginalized because 'their feminine bodies are out of place'. Pullen and Simpson (2009, p. 561, emphasis added), in their research on men working as nurses and primary school teachers also highlight how, in these occupations, 'men are often seen as not only a minority to women . . . *but also their Other*'. They show some of the complex ways in which men 'manage' difference, and in doing so transcend their Otherness, by doing masculinity and appropriating femininity in ways that simultaneously subvert and maintain gender hierarchies.

Much of this scholarship has concerned itself with the social and organizational construction of gender, and with the perpetuation of inequalities based on gender difference. In this respect, de Beauvoir's writing encourages us to develop more theoretically sophisticated accounts of Othering as a process of organization, understanding not only how we are embedded within organizational structures that serve to disadvantage, discriminate, marginalize and negate, but also why, and with what consequences. The processual ontology underpinning her work requires us to consider the dynamic relationship between how, as situated subjects, we are positioned organizationally. Her situated understanding of becoming requires us to confront the conditions of possibility that compel and constrain that becoming, focusing critical attention on the terms of recognition, and on the consequences of mis-recognition, and particularly, on the processes through which organizations exploit our desire for recognition. In this respect, de Beauvoir's understanding of the need for recognition as the most basic human premise leads her to emphasize how our mutual inter-dependence, while not a form of subjugation in and of itself (quite the contrary), can provide the basis for it: 'It is this interdependence which explains why oppression is possible and why it is so hateful' (de Beauvoir, 1976, p. 82). We turn, now, to consider a recent case of gender discrimination within organizational life that both illustrates some of the theoretical ideas considered thus far, and which can be understood with reference to these, particularly de Beauvoir's critique of women's situated, embodied Otherness.

Women being brought to heel: the PwC case

In December 2015, Nicola Thorp, a woman working as a receptionist at PwC's offices in London, was sent home without pay for refusing to wear high-heeled shoes.[5] Thorp was told that the smart, flat shoes she was wearing did not comply with her employer's specific requirement for women to wear shoes with a heel height of between two and four inches.

In response, Thorp started an online petition calling for it to be made 'illegal for a company to require women to wear high heels at work',[6] which was signed by over 150,000 people. This prompted a governmental inquiry that included the testimonies of hundreds of women and expert witnesses from trade unions, political groups and professional bodies. Collectively, these witnesses provided evidence of the pain and damage caused by wearing high-heeled shoes for long periods of time. During the course of the inquiry, it became clear that the problem was by no means an individual one, or one confined to shoes. Women reported being told to dye their hair a particular colour, to wear revealing clothing, and to regularly reapply a minimum amount of make-up. (No men came forward to say that the same rules, or even informal pressures, applied to them.)

The report acknowledges that legislation is already in place (in the form of the Equality Act 2010 in the UK, and in similar legislation in many other countries) that should prevent such forms of discrimination. Yet continuing to treat men and women's bodies differently in the workplace has many potential benefits for employers. The Fawcett Society emphasized this in their contribution to the inquiry, highlighting the extent to which sexualized dress codes telling a woman that how she looks is more important than what she says or does is a good way to justify paying her less (Hancock and Tyler, 2017).

As Bell (2016) has written, however, high heels are powerful, fetishized symbols in our society, signifying the seductive power attributed to women, particularly in the media. As she puts it, they are 'a marker of high status, despite their impracticality and the physical strain that they put on a woman's body'. It is precisely this double-bind that de Beauvoir helps us to make sense of – heeled shoes are part of what she calls 'the drama of woman'; they maintain 'the feminine mystique' and epitomize women's ambivalent relationship to our bodies. This particular case also provides an important example of how, through the organization of gender, women's position as the second sex is maintained; organizations literally keep women in their place through controlling their bodies, and through the maintenance of appearance norms that serve to perpetuate a series of constraints and compulsions governing recognition. By wearing heels, women are deemed to evoke power, respect and admiration through a form that ironically, and painfully, undermines their capacity to meaningfully experience any of these; as women's bodies continue to be manipulated and reduced to aesthetic objects in the labour market women's position as Other is affirmed, as they are deemed unworthy of or incapable of providing recognition other than as display objects.

Concluding thoughts

Re-engaging de Beauvoir's writing in order to develop a feminist critique of these kinds of organizational practices has the potential to enable us to understand, on the one hand, the role that organizations play in compelling us to become in particular ways and, on the other, the organizational constraints limiting this becoming, itself a process of organization. De

Beauvoir reminds us that not only how we become who we are, but also why, is driven by ontological desire – by the basic, human need for recognition of oneself as a viable subject – and furthermore, because both the desire for recognition and the conditions of viability governing its conferral or denial are always socially situated, the process through which we become who we are is organized in such a way as to relegate women to a perpetually secondary, mis-recognized, status. Understood through this 'organizational' lens, situating women as Other constitutes a fundamentally organizational process at both a social and ontological level.

Notes

1 As Marshall (2000, p. 169) has put it, both the substance and the form of de Beauvoir's work serves as a poignant reminder to us that 'the personal, professional and intellectual are interwoven'.

2 As Margaret Simons (2015) has written in her introduction to a recent collection, even though much has been written about de Beauvoir and her life, periodic discoveries of unpublished drafts and letters continue to provide new insights and surprises.

3 The political Left accused de Beauvoir of deviating from the real political struggle by focusing specifically on 'the woman question', whilst also arguing that, as a relatively privileged member of the Parisian intellectual elite, she could not possibly claim to speak on behalf of ordinary women (Jardine, 1979). From the Right, de Beauvoir endured more personal attacks, being daubed both a pornographer because of her graphic depictions of women's bodies and references to sexuality, and amoral because of her own (and espoused) rejection of marriage and motherhood. As Schwarzer (1984) notes, even Camus (a personal friend of both de Beauvoir and Sartre, and a member of their intellectual circle) stated publicly that de Beauvoir had made a laughing stock of the French male by publishing *The Second Sex*. A further attack came from the claim that is was actually Sartre who had written much of the text, a critique that seems to have taken de Beauvoir rather too literally when she described herself as 'Sartre's disciple in matters philosophical' (see Jardine, 1979).

4 De Beauvoir draws heavily here on Sartre's notion of 'facticity'.

5 Nicola Thorp was employed by an agency, Portico, which describes itself as a 'specialist provider of high quality, tailored front and back of house guest services' (Portico website, 'About Us', cited in House of Commons report, *High Heels and Workplace Dress Codes*. 25 January 2017, page 4).

6 House of Commons report, *High Heels and Workplace Dress Codes*. 25 January 2017, page 4.

Recommended reading

Original text by de Beauvoir

de Beauvoir, S. (2011). First published 1949. *The second sex*. Trans. C. Borde, and S. Malovany-Chevallier. London: Vintage.

Key academic text

Marshall, J. (2000). Revisiting Simone de Beauvoir: Recognizing feminist contributions to pluralism in organizational studies. *Journal of Management Inquiry*, 9(2), pp. 166–172.

Accessible resource

Moi, T. (1994). *Simone de Beauvoir: The making of an intellectual woman*. Oxford: Blackwell.

References

Ahmed, S. (2006). *Queer phenomenology*. London: Duke University Press.

Ahmed, S. (2017). *Living a feminist life*. London: Duke University Press.

Bell, E. (2016). Wearing heels to work is a game women have been losing for decades. *The Conversation*, 13 May 2016.

Bolton, S. (2005). Women's work, dirty work: The gynaecology nurse as other. *Gender, Work and Organization*, 12(2), pp. 169–186.

Butler, J. (1990). *Gender trouble*. London: Routledge.

Butler, J. (2004). *Undoing gender*. London: Routledge.

Butler, J. (2005). *Giving an account of oneself*. London: Routledge.

Calás, M. and Smircich, L. (2000). Ignored for 'Good Reason': Beauvoir's philosophy as a revision of social identity approaches. *Journal of Management Inquiry*, 9(2), pp. 193–199.

Cixous, H. (1986). *The newly born woman*. Trans. B. Wing. Minneapolis, MN: University of Minnesota Press.

Czarniawska, B. (2006). Doing gender unto the other: Fiction as a mode of studying gender discrimination in organizations. *Gender, Work and Organization*, 13(3), pp. 234–253.

de Beauvoir, S. (2000). First published 1948. *The ethics of ambiguity*. Trans. B. Frechtman. New York, NY: Citadel Press.

de Beauvoir, S. (1984). First published 1943. *She came to stay*. Trans. Y. Moyse, and R. Senhouse. London: Flamingo.

de Beauvoir, S. (1985). First published 1981. *Adieux*. Trans. P. O'Brian. Harmondsworth: Penguin.

de Beauvoir, S. (1988). First published 1949. *The second sex*. Trans. H. M. Parshley. London: Jonathan Cape.

de Beauvoir, S. (1996). First published 1972. *The coming of age*. Trans. P. O'Brian. London: Norton.

de Beauvoir, S. (2011). First published 1949. *The second sex*. Trans. C. Borde, and S. Malovany-Chevallier. London: Vintage.

Duchen, C. (1986). *Feminism in France*. London: Routledge.

Evans, M. (1996). *Simone de Beauvoir*. London: Sage.

Gherardi, S. (1996). Gendered organizational cultures: Narratives of women travellers in a male world. *Gender, Work and Organization*, 3(4), pp. 187–201.

Hancock, P. and Tyler, M. (2007). Undoing gender and the aesthetics of organizational performance. *Gender, Work and Organization*, 16(6), pp. 512–533.

Hancock, P. and Tyler, M. (2017). How discriminatory dress codes at work are digging their heels in. *The Conversation*, 30 January 2017.

Hegel, G. W. F. (1979). First published 1807. *Phenomenology of spirit*. Trans. A. V. Miller. Oxford: Oxford University Press.

Höpfl, H. (2011). Women's writing. In: E. Jeanes, D. Knights, and P. Yancey Martin, eds., *Handbook of gender, work and organization*. Oxford: Wiley.

Jardine, A. (1979). An interview with Simone de Beauvoir. *Signs: Journal of Women in Culture and Society*, 5(2), pp. 224–236.

Jeanes, E. (2007). The doing and undoing of gender: The importance of being a credible female victim. *Gender, Work and Organization*, 14(6), pp. 552–571.

Kerfoot, D. and Knights, D. (1998). Managing masculinity in contemporary organizational life: A man(agerial) project. *Organization*, 5(1), pp. 7–26.

Kerfoot, D. and Knights, D. (2004). Between representations and subjectivity: Gender binaries and the politics of organizational transformation. *Gender, Work and Organization*, 11(4), pp. 430–454.

Kruks, S. (1992). Gender and subjectivity: Simone de Beauvoir and contemporary feminism. *Signs: Journal of Women in Culture and Society*, 18(1), pp. 89–110.

Kruks, S. (2001). *Retrieving experience*. London: Cornell University Press.

Kruks, S. (2012). *Simone de Beauvoir and the politics of ambiguity*. Oxford: Oxford University Press.

Marshall, J. (2000). Revisiting Simone de Beauvoir: Recognizing feminist contributions to pluralism in organizational studies. *Journal of Management Inquiry*, 9(2), pp. 166–172.

Martin, P. Y. (2003). 'Said and Done' versus 'Saying and Doing': Gendering practices, practicing gender at work. *Gender and Society*, 17(3), pp. 342–366.

Martin, P. Y. (2006). Practising gender at work: Further thoughts on reflexivity. *Gender, Work and Organization*, 13(3), pp. 254–276.

Mavin, S. and Grandy, G. (2016). A theory of abject appearance: Women elite leaders' intra-gender 'Management' of bodies and appearance. *Human Relations*, 69(5), pp. 1095–1120.

Merleau Ponty, M. (2002). First published 1948. *Phenomenology of perception*. London: Routledge.

Moi, T. (1994). *Simone de Beauvoir: The making of an intellectual woman*. Oxford: Blackwell.

Phillips, M. and Knowles, D. (2012). Performance and performativity: Undoing fictions of women business owners. *Gender, Work and Organization*, 19(4), pp. 416–437.

Powell, A., Bagilhole, B. and Dainty, A. (2009). How women engineers do and undo gender: Consequences for gender equality. *Gender, Work and Organization*, 16(4), pp. 411–428.

Pullen, A. (2006). Gendering the research self: Social practice and corporeal multiplicity in the writing of organizational research. *Gender, Work and Organization*, 13(3), pp. 277–298.

Pullen, A. and Knights, D. (2007). Editorial: Undoing gender – Organizing and disorganizing performance. *Gender, Work and Organization*, 14(6), pp. 505–511.

Pullen, A. and Simpson, R. (2009). Managing difference in feminized work: Men, otherness and social practice. *Human Relations*, 62(4), pp. 561–587.

Rowbotham, S. (2009). '*Foreword*' to the second sex. Trans. C. Borde, and S. Malovany-Chevallier. London: Vintage, pp. ix–xix.

Schwarzer, A. (1984). *After the second sex: Conversations with de Beauvoir*. London: Pantheon.

Simons, M. (2015). Introduction. In: S. de Beauvoir, and M. Simons, eds., *Feminist writings*. Chicago, IL: University of Illinois Press.

Simpson, R. (2011). Men discussing women and women discussing men: Reflexivity, transformation and gendered practice in the context of nursing care. *Gender, Work and Organization*, 18(4), pp. 377–398.

Swan, E. (2017). What are white people to do? Listening, challenging ignorance, generous encounters and the 'not yet' as diversity research praxis. *Gender, Work and Organization*, 25(5), pp. 547–563.

Tyler, M. (2014). Simone de Beauvoir. In: J. Helin, T. Hernes, D. Hjorth, and R. Holt, eds., *The Oxford handbook of philosophy and organisation studies*. Oxford: Oxford University Press, pp. 396–412.

West, C. and Zimmerman, D. (1987). Doing gender. *Gender & Society*, 1(2), pp. 125–151.

4 Julia Kristeva

Speaking of the body to understand the language of organizations

Marianna Fotaki

Julia Kristeva is a Bulgarian-born, French poststructuralist philosopher, semiotician, literary critic and psychoanalyst whose rich and diverse work spans five decades. Her ideas on the body and the abjection of the maternal have had a profound influence on developing feminist thought. She has written extensively about language, drawing attention to movements within text and its intersection with the real, material body. In groundbreaking explorations of otherness, Kristeva provides theoretical foundations to explain various forms of social exclusion and how these can be overcome. Her influence thus extends beyond feminism, and she continues to be very productive. Recently, Kristeva examined the nature of the female genius in biographies of philosopher Hannah Arendt, child psychoanalyst and founder of object relations theory Melanie Klein and French writer Colette. She intervenes in key public debates on contemporary political issues such as terrorism, and also writes fiction.

Kristeva is now Professor Emeritus at the University of Paris VII Diderot and holds honorary degrees from universities around the world. She has received many international prizes, including Officer of the French Legion of Honour (the highest accolade in France) in 1997 and the prestigious Hannah Arendt Prize for Political Thought in 2006. In 2004 she was the first person to be awarded Norway's Prix Holberg in recognition of her 'innovative explorations of questions on the intersection of language, culture and literature which inspired research across the humanities and the social sciences throughout the world and have also had a significant impact on feminist theory' (www.holbergprisen.no/en/julia-kristeva.html). In 2008 she established the Simone de Beauvoir Prize for Women's Freedom.

In presenting her work, this chapter portrays a woman writer and intellectual who lives her theory by taking inspiration from her own embodied experience. Kristeva's thinking is strongly influenced by her position as a foreign woman and a hybrid subject building bridges across various disciplines. This has also allowed her to establish herself as a global thinker.

The chapter provides an account of the influence of Kristeva's theorization on management and organization studies, which has been considerably under-utilized and is probably among her least important contributions. Specifically, it focuses on the role of the body and language in constituting subjectivity. I briefly present these ideas before moving on to the concept of abjection, and how this has been taken in organization studies and management. The chapter concludes by discussing the notion of 'the stranger within ourselves' in the context of othering in contemporary organizations and society.

The textual and material body

Kristeva arrived in France in the 1960s, when grand poststructuralist theorists (Jacques Derrida, Michel Foucault and Roland Barthes) were about to launch their revolution in social sciences, arts and humanities. Tzvetan Todorov, a Bulgarian literary critic, introduced her to these circles and to the work of Mikhail Bakhtin, a Soviet linguist of the 1930s. These encounters were crucial to Kristeva's development as a theorist of the semiotic. She offered 'semanalysis' as a way of revealing movements of the signifying process in the text. Through 'intertextuality', another term inspired by Bakhtin, she proposed to explicate how different texts cross within a text, and how competing discourses elide and modify a single text.

Kristeva advanced her theory on the process of signification in language by proposing that it is constituted of two different but interacting elements: the symbolic, associated with its cognitive, discursive and normative aspects; and the semiotic, preverbal rhythms of the body underlying this, which she called the 'chora'. The chora, a term borrowed from Plato, describes an essential aspect of subjectivity that pre-exists symbolization and is associated with the maternal body.

Kristeva evocatively describes the chora as a sort of 'dancing body' (from the Greek *khoreia*, meaning 'dance') in perpetual motion. She claims that, just as dance allows the dancer to explore an infinite chain of body movements, the chora energizes the sign (as well as the subject) by placing expulsion at the core of its structure. Through such movements, expulsion rejects a linear division between signifier and signified and 'the dissolution of the subject as signifying subject', as well as 'any partitions in which the subject might shelter in order to constitute itself' (Kristeva, 1998, p. 134).

Although she links the chora with the maternal, as the site where such rhythms originate, it is not situated in any specific body. This means that both men and women have access to the semiotic, and the semiotic chora has infinite potential to create signifying movements and is 'a multiplicity of ex-pulsions, ensuring its infinite renewal' (Kristeva, 1998, p. 134). The implication of the body becoming the locus of the semiotic chora – the place of perpetual renewal in the signifying process that encompasses both being and becoming – is important for how the subject is able to represent itself.

One implication of Kristeva's theorization on subjectivity is that it allows us to reject any constancy or unifying position of the unconscious/conscious or signifier/signified, because unity of the subject, sign or language does not exist. For Kristeva, the subject emerges from movements of the preverbal chora and cannot have a stable entity; it exists only in the process of becoming: 'The process dissolves the linguistic sign and its system (word, syntax), dissolves, that is, even the earliest and most solid guarantee of the unitary subject' (Kristeva, 1998, p. 134). Kristeva's semiological investigation into human subjectivity thus shifts from a functional, homogenic and homological account of the symbolic order (the realm of the 'unitary', independent subject) to the unstable yet indissoluble relationship between the heterogeneous domains of the symbolic and the semiotic.

These ideas formed part of Kristeva's early work in the 1960s and '70s, including her path-breaking doctoral thesis, *La Révolution du langage poétique*, which was first published in French in 1974 (*Revolution in Poetic Language*, published in English in 1985) and was her magnum opus that earned her a full professorship in French academia, as well as the largely untranslated *Sémiotikè: recherches pour une sémanalyse* (1969) and *Polylogue* (1977). During this period, she was actively involved in writing for and then editing the avant-garde literary magazine *Tel Quel*.

The core contribution of these works is to bring the living body back into language. The Kristevan symbolic is both the rhythms of the body and language; it exists through their intersection and by bringing these two into 'dialogue' with each other. The fundamentally dialogic structure of subjectivity comprising body/language also foregrounds a psychoanalytic understanding of the subject's becoming that originates in the unconscious:

> This is because we may indeed affirm that *in the beginning was the word*, but before the beginning there was the unconscious with its repressed content.
>
> (Kristeva, 2004, italics in the original)

Overall, Kristeva proposes a nuanced theory of subjectivity that is both processual and defined by embodiment. I now turn to discussing how she integrates psychoanalysis with linguistics to theorize the process of becoming an enfleshed subject.

Subject as flesh in language

Jacques Lacan, who read psychoanalysis through a linguistic prism, was a close friend of Kristeva (and, according to some accounts, also her psychoanalyst). His interpretation of Sigmund Freud's theory of drives exerted a profound influence on Kristeva's writings in the 1980s. Following her own psychoanalytic training, she elaborated on the relationship between semiotic drives and symbolic language in the trilogy *Powers of Horror* (1982), *Tales of Love* (1987) and *Black Sun* (1989). These three volumes, respectively offer original and powerful theories of abjection, love and depression.

Under the influence of Lacan's work, Kristeva links the evolution of the subject to the evolution of language, focusing specifically on ways in which the subject enters into the realm of the symbolic order. While she accepts the key Lacanian premise that we only exist as speaking subjects, the Kristevan symbolic order (and therefore signification) is not only defined by the meaning function of language. Instead, she proposes a more complex theory of signification, weaving together both semiotic and symbolic elements. She reintroduces the power of the body as semiotic chora, which underlies the symbolic realm of language and culture, softening aspects of Freudian and Lacanian psychoanalysis that exclude women. By stressing the role of the maternal in the formation of subjectivity, the Kristevan body becomes a source of its own signification as a site where meaning emerges. In her later work on otherness, presented in the second part of this chapter, Kristeva (1991) specifically demonstrates that whereas a Lacanian re-reading of Freud's work conceives woman as a lack and a void, equating her with the negative and death itself, this is incomplete because it ignores the semiotic body as foundational to signification.

Next I discuss the notion of abjection, which has been influential in feminist theory, social sciences, cultural studies and arts, and what it means to be abjected in organizations and society. I refer only briefly to Kristeva's other works of this period to elucidate these arguments.

Abjection

In *Powers of Horror: Essay on Abjection* (1982), Kristeva focuses on the significance of the maternal and pre-oedipal, conventionally associated in psychoanalytic thinking with the stages of prelingual, and therefore presocial, development, which she locates in the rhythm of the body that she calls the semiotic chora. As discussed above, the semiotic chora 'is no more than the place where the subject is both generated and negated, the place where his unity succumbs before the process of charges and stases that produce him' (Kristeva, 1986, p. 95).

While asserting the importance of the symbolic order (and language) for subjectivity formation, Kristeva explains how, during the individuation process, 'the child learns to repel and reject parts of the self that are associated with the feminine, which becomes the abject' (1982, p. 171). Abjection is necessarily directed at the maternal body, which is the locus of the undifferentiated fusion of object/subject existing in the state of presubjectivity. As Kristeva notes:

> Abjection preserves what existed in the archaism of pre-objectal relationship, in the immemorial violence with which a body becomes separated from another body in order to be.
>
> (Kristeva, 1982, p. 10)

Abjection is a theoretical concept taken from anthropology, inspired by Mary Douglas's (1966) work on specific communal rules established to separate pure from dangerous substances often associated with bodily functions. By rendering a substance or its use impure, we are socially conditioned to experience revulsion and disgust on encountering or even imagining 'the abjected' (person, activity, object). For Kristeva, abjection acquires broader political significance and metaphorical meaning, and is associated with exclusion/inclusion as the foundation of the subject's social existence. Specifically, abjection enables her to consider ways of establishing boundaries between the individual and the social body. Kristeva also renders abjection intrinsic to any act of artistic creation, which she links to emergence from a state of semi-psychotic undifferentiation and the subject's journey towards individuation. Violent separation from maternal fusion therefore becomes inevitable if we are to avoid a psychotic collapse of meaning: 'Matricide is our vital necessity, the sine qua non condition of our individuation' (Kristeva, 1989, p. 38).

This linking of psychosis to inability to separate from the mother (in *The Black Sun*, 1989) and matricide as a precondition for becoming a viable subject have raised objections from feminists. For instance, Imogen Tyler (2009) argues persuasively against recasting all forms of abjection as re-enactments of the primary matricide, 'an act that haunts the subject "unflaggingly, like an inescapable boomerang"' (Kristeva, 1982, p. 1, in Tyler, 2009). Citing Judith Butler, Tyler objects to the definition of abjection as a primary cause rather than the product of a specific discourse that has a negative effect on women. Tyler's related political objection is that it ignores the living histories of violence towards real maternal bodies that are integral to processes of abjection. Conflating the maternal body with presubjectivity necessitating her abjection is therefore unfortunate, as is reiterating the abjection of her body as an integral psychic process, because it is often misdirected to all women, whether or not they are mothers (Oliver, 1993; see also Fotaki, 2011 for an organizational example in academic settings). In her essay on abjection (1982), Kristeva explains that the root cause of abjection is a product of the patriarchal symbolic. She posits that the representation of woman as mother, particularly evident in Western tradition, excludes the possibility of woman from the symbolic, because in patriarchal societies the social is essentially defined by repressing maternal authority. Because of this, she maintains, our society places the female subject in a double bind. The oppressive condition of the (m)Other (as the unknowable and irreconcilable other) in the Lacanian symbolic leaves the undesirable option of either mother-identification or father-identification. A woman's situation is complex because, if she identifies with the mother, she ensures her exclusion from and marginality in relation to the patriarchal order. She therefore carries the mother within her as a 'living corpse', the mother's body that no longer nourishes. Yet, if a woman identifies with the father and makes herself in his image, she ends up becoming him and supporting the same patriarchal order. This excludes and marginalizes herself as woman, and also forms a defence against her mother.

While Kristeva holds patriarchy responsible for women's diminished position, and uses her theory of abjection to elucidate the process through which this is achieved, she often privileges the conceptual maternal body rather than the literal feminine body. This body is resolutely positioned outside the realm of symbolic language. The conception of motherhood and what it stands for in the patriarchal discourse is thus often used figuratively. The maternal body, Kristeva argues, is determinedly preverbal, which explains why the physical body is idealized (as virginal, for instance) or otherwise cast away in the patriarchal symbolic order. In *Stabat Mater* (1986, p. 176), exploring the relationship between mother and religious belief, she states:

> Every God, even including the God of the Word, relies on mother Goddess. Christianity is perhaps also the last of the religions to have displayed in broad light the bipolar structure of belief: on·the one hand, the difficult experience of the Word . . . on the other, the reassuring wrapping in the proverbial mirage of the mother.

In other words, the Virgin Mary in Christianity is indispensable for the paternal Christian discourse. 'In the beginning was the Word', and it could not have existed without its underpinning links to the maternal: 'Christians must have found such a postulate sufficiently hard to believe [that] they added its compensation, its permanent lining: the maternal receptacle, purified as it might have been by virginal fantasy' (Jonte-Pace, 1992, pp. 175–176).

In making these connections, Kristeva elucidates why the speaking female subject exists uneasily in the symbolic order (and occupies an unstable speaking position), encounters difficulty in taking up this position. Her foothold in the symbolic order is difficult and precarious because she must constantly recreate forms of identification with this order, against the background of her own demands and desires. Kristeva urges women to reject this dilemma: they must neither refuse to enter the symbolic order nor adopt the masculine model of femininity:

> Let us refuse both these extremes. . . . By listening; by recognizing the unspoken in all discourse, however Revolutionary, by emphasizing at each point whatever remains unsatisfied, repressed, new, eccentric, incomprehensible, that which disturbs the mutual understanding of the established powers.
>
> (Kristeva, 1986, p. 156)

Feminist or not, and does this matter?

Kristeva's work has inspired developments in feminist thinking, and has advanced our understanding of how gender works in organizations and society. While her ideas about the maternal as pre-lingual have often divided feminists, many have turned for inspiration to her theory of the body. This is because Kristeva's work offers ways of rehabilitating the body as the locus of the semiotic chora where language and subjectivity originates, since it 'logically and chronologically precedes the establishment of the symbolic and its subject' (Kristeva, 1982, p. 41). Specifically, she reintroduces the semiotic musicality and rhythms of the body as co-existing with the meaning in language, in a dialectical as well as dialogical relationship inspired by Bakhtin (Edelstein, 1992): 'these two modalities are inseparable within the *signifying process* that constitutes language' (Kristeva, 1982, p. 24; italics in the original). On the other hand, concept of abjection explains the repulsion and disgust that the body generates in patriarchal societies. Kristeva's theoretical developments, of the maternal as an impure body and the feminine as absent from the realm of symbolic language and culture, have been used extensively to explain various forms of misogyny in society (Tyler, 2009) and the exclusion of women in organizations (Phillips and Rippin, 2010; Fotaki, 2011; 2012; 2013; Rizq, 2013; Gatrell, 2017), as discussed in the next section.

Yet Kristeva does not consider herself a feminist. This is for two related reasons. The first is that, according to her, we are born into a patriarchal world where signification occurs within its limits. Entering into the symbolic governed by the Law of Father (a terminology she borrows from Lacan) must therefore occur within its rules as a condition for women's intelligibility. As Gambaudo (2017) puts it: 'In a world where cultural organization is, by and large, founded upon patriarchal experience, the ordering of meaning is necessarily mediated by patriarchal rule'. In other words, women cannot change the patriarchal rules without losing their intelligibility. This can also explain the tensions between her conceptions of motherhood and language following opposite trajectories (Höpfl, 2000). In the *Stabat Mater*, Höpfl indicates for instance, 'She constructs the text from two positions, her own formal writing on the Virgin Mary and her personal reflections on Motherhood in dialectical opposition' (Ibid.: 99). Finding a female counterpart to the phallic symbol is ineffective for Kristeva. Following from this, she argues that feminism aims to displace the hegemonic patriarchal discourse by offering a reversal of this discourse, without questioning its rules as this would be antithetical to the process of signification. The feminist tendency to promote female autonomy thus merely echoes hegemonic constructs 'where being an autonomous subject is a masculine cultural prerogative from which women have already been excluded' (Baxter, 2003, p. 35). This is her second objection relating to feminism.

In her essay on feminism, 'Woman's Time' (1986, p. 208), she compares radical feminism with religion, stating that 'in this context its religious dimensions make it dangerous', while envisaging a different type of feminism which is not based on reversal but has the capacity to

> channel this demand for the difference into each and every element of the female whole, and finally, bring out the singularity of each woman, and beyond this, her multiplicities, plural languages, beyond the horizon, beyond sight, beyond faith itself.
>
> (Ibid.)

To do this, women must take up their rightful places in the symbolic. Rather than doing away with the symbolic order, women must place themselves within it. The way forward for women entails both recognition of the Freudian law of castration, which establishes sexual difference as the organizing principle of Western patriarchy, and the Lacanian Law of the Father that constitutes us as subjects (for further discussion, see Fotaki and Harding, 2013; 2017, chap. 3). In order not to be trapped by an oppressive double bind of identity, women must express their *jouissance* (denoting enjoyment and painful pleasure that relates to desire in Lacanian terminology) within the symbolic order without relinquishing any of their difference. Women must take up their identity as an identity *in process* (via the semiotic) in order not to be linked with that identity in an oppressive way.

Kristeva also argues that it is necessary for women to find an alternative psychic register beyond the rules of patriarchy if they are to summon their own truth. Such truth is to be found in semiotic motility, which has the capacity 'to disrupt the strict symbolic order' (Moi, 1988, p. 170). Yet it is only through language, which is by nature symbolic, that women can hope to challenge the law of patriarchy and create new discourses. For Kristeva, no 'woman writing' is possible outside the symbolic framework. In the current economy, there is no other space from which the woman can speak. If she is able to speak at all, it must be within the framework of symbolic language. The aim of woman writing is 'to explore the relationship between something we call "woman" and phallocentric intelligibility' (Gambaudo, 2017); yet her privileging of the symbolic order and her description of the maternal as subordinated helps to consolidate the power of the paternal (Butler, 1989). This is further reiterated, as Butler suggests, in Kristeva's use of psychoanalysis to narrow the embodied experience, rendering lesbianism culturally unintelligible.

More promising is Kristeva's argument for a need to retain the symbolic as the domain of language and of love (Kristeva, 1987), which signifies 'openness to the other, and it is what gives me my human dimension' (Kristeva, 1980, p. 144, cited in Oliver, 1993). I shall discuss this in the penultimate section of this chapter after tracing the influence of Kristeva's theorization of abjection on organization studies and management.

Abjection of the body in organizations

Abjection has been one of Kristeva's most influential ideas (another is intertextuality) that has travelled across social sciences, arts and humanities. It provides a vocabulary for many feminist analyses that explain the unequal and inferior position of women in society. It is also used to discuss the exclusion of different groups of people from the social body.

Organizational scholars have employed the idea of abjection for both of these purposes to theorize women's discrimination in organizations (Fotaki, 2009a; 2011; 2013) and how it may affect female employees tasked with reproducing the abjected form of femininity, for instance in the media (Hunter and Kivinen, 2017). The concept of abjection has also been used to identify inadmissible forms of work, including sex work (Tyler, 2011), and mental health patients who are treated as abject in the NHS (Rizq, 2013), as well as historical examples of abjection such as the institutionalization of poor children born out of wedlock in pre-war Ireland (Kenny, 2016). Organizational scholars have also used abjection productively to reintegrate the excluded experience of suffering in the Holocaust (Sørensen, 2014), and the trauma of being rejected (Fotaki, 2012) or excluded (Gatrell, 2017) in the workplace.

In my own work, I have drawn on Kristeva's theorization on the symbolic and textual representation of woman as abject to explain the difficult position of women in academia as speaking subjects. I argue that her explication of the double bind in which women find themselves in the patriarchal symbolic order (for further discussion, see also Oliver, 1993) helps us to understand the ambiguity of women's 'writing from the body' (see also Fotaki and Harding, 2017, chap. 6), relegating them to the position of non-speaking subject. This is because whenever an (academic) woman identifies with assigned feminine (maternal) roles, she ensures her exclusion from, and marginality within, the patriarchal order (Kristeva, 1982). She thus colludes in her own exclusion (for further discussion, see Fotaki, 2012). Another related consequence of abjection is both overt and covert refusal to recognize women as producers of knowledge in academia, and their association with nature or the sexualized body (see Fotaki, 2011). This, I suggest, causes them to be cast away least they disrupt the symbolic (masculine) order from within. In my empirical work on women in UK business and management schools, I offer examples of how representation of the real (and imagined) non-phallic (female) body leads to women's exclusion from the process of knowledge creation in an attempt to keep it pure and uncontaminated by atheoretical and embodied writing (Fotaki, 2009a; 2011). Women often become caught in a double bind of a more practical nature: they are aware that they do not help their careers by conforming to the demands of the patriarchal symbolic order of academia by 'acting as men', yet they feel they cannot do otherwise.

Researchers have explored gendered forms of abjection in other contexts, and have transposed this concept to understand how abjection manifests itself in various organizational and work settings. Hunter and Kivinen (2017) examine how women themselves may construct abjection in a work environment where women dominate the workforce and where the product (pre-teen and teenage magazines for girls) is highly gendered. Gatrell (2017) uses Kristeva's idea to advance a contemporary theory of 'abjection as practice' in relation to breastfeeding and employment, in terms of a purposeful intent to exclude breast milk production from workplace contexts.

Other researchers support the idea of Kristevan abjection through Butler's theoretical apparatus, explaining how individuals' desire for recognition subjects them to compliance with social norms in order to become intelligible, even if these norms are injurious to themselves (Butler, 1997). Like women, individuals who violate socially accepted norms, such as the terms that make up their own gender (Butler, 2004, p. 31), are marginalized as abject and excluded from the patriarchal symbolic. Kenny (2010; 2012) examines these issues in the context of development work, demonstrating how the fear of abjection causes people to conform to organizational demands to maintain a desirable identity. In her later work, she uses abjection to explore the role of organizations in the perpetration of large-scale violence, and ways of legitimating this violence by constructing subjects as abject boundary objects in extreme cases, such as children in Ireland's industrial schools (Kenny, 2016). Finally, in a study of UK public mental health services, Rizq (2013) explores they ways in which contemporary preoccupations with regulation, surveillance and governance in large public institutions such as the NHS for instance, may be characterized by symbolic attempts to gain mastery over feelings unconsciously deemed to be abject reminders of the body in the case of mental health patients.

Making different categories of people abject is an important aspect of Kristeva's central preoccupation with the idea of otherness as the foundation of social and communal life (Kristeva, 1991). Her path-breaking contribution has been to cast, as prototypical of all forms of exclusion, the abjection of the maternal body that has been projected onto women throughout patriarchal history, and the feeling of being 'a matter out of place' that this continues to evoke in culture, society and politics, with multiple consequences. This is because abjection refers to the ostensibly inexplicable sense of horror experienced when the boundary between self and other is in danger of dissolution. In a broader sense, the term refers to the process through which identificatory regimes exclude subjects by rendering them unintelligible or beyond classification. As such, the abjection of others serves to maintain or reinforce boundaries that are threatened (Phillips, 2014). While otherness or foreignness are not synonymous with abjection, both concepts are concerned with boundary, in this case separating the inner and outer and who is to be included/excluded from a given social group, as I shall discuss next.

Strangers in ourselves

In her book *Strangers to Ourselves*, Julia Kristeva puts forward the concept of the foreigner as 'the one who does not belong to the group, who is not "one of them", the other', suggesting that 'the foreigner, as it has often been noted, can only be defined in negative fashion' (Kristeva, 1991, p. 95). She often refers to her own experience of foreignness: 'One may feel *more* of a foreigner in France than in any other country, but at the same time one is *better* as a foreigner in France than in any other country' (Kristeva, 2004). Yet psychoanalytic theory provides her with pertinent insights into the difficulty of dealing with the foreign other. According to Freud (1919), this originates in the *Unheimlich*, the 'uncanny strangeness' of the unconscious, and our tendency to escape from it. Kristeva (1991) notes that woman's maternal body is seen as the primary site arousing a feeling of the 'uncanny' in Freudian psychoanalysis. Although Freud acknowledged woman's body as 'the place that each one of us lived once upon a time and in the beginning' (Freud, 1919, p. 245), he also declared this 'place' to be the source of the strange feeling of the uncanny that the foreigner inspires in us. As Kristeva (1991, p. 185) states:

> In the fascinated rejection that the foreigner arouses in us, there is a share of uncanny strangeness in the sense that Freud discovered in it, and which takes again our infantile desires and fears of the other – the other of death, the other of woman, the other of uncontrollable drive. The foreigner is within us.

Since, in Kristeva's words, 'the foreigner is within us', its status loses the particularity of a national or racial definition and becomes a universal state of the psyche (Kristeva, 1991, p. 181). But this psychic reality is then extended to the realm of the symbolic. She pointedly argues:

> My discontent in living with the other – my strangeness, his strangeness – rests on the perturbed logic that governs this strange bundle of drive and language, of nature and symbol, constituted by the unconscious, *always already shaped by the other*.
>
> (Kristeva, 1991, p. 182, my emphasis)

In offering the concept of the other as linked to the uncanny of the unintelligible unconscious, Kristeva provides new ways of theorizing on various forms of difference as a structural aspect of the inalienable otherness of the human psyche. Her theorization builds on Freud's concept of the 'uncanny strangeness' of the unconscious, where the repressed fearful, painful or unacceptable parts of ourselves reside, to suggest how various 'others' bring these up. Her argument is twofold. On the one hand, the unconscious that can never be fully comprehended and symbolized reminds us of 'not being at home', which makes us forever estranged from ourselves. On the other hand, the 'othered' and dehumanized bearers of our abjection reinforce this feeling of strangeness and foreignness in ourselves, as they remind us of our worst fears about survivability and being cast away from the social. This is because the most deep-seated unconscious fear, which we try to suppress without ever fully succeeding, is the fear of death and annihilation.

The 'otherness' of our unconscious that we cannot bear in ourselves is then externalized onto various groups of conceptual 'others' (such as women throughout history, and Jews in Christian tradition). Various ideological, religious and social discourses are then mobilized to justify and normalize this. In her discussion of the idealized female central to patriarchy for instance, Kristeva stresses the links between motherhood, religion and death (Jonte-Pace, 1992, p. 9) in explaining why woman's body must be exiled from the symbolic.

Yet intersubjectivity, or the acceptance of the other, is inescapable for Kristeva; it is part of the structure of language, and language is at the core of the symbolization process. Kristeva (1991, p. 180) follows Lacan's position on the 'unconscious structured as language' in stating that

> the localization of foreignness thus recognized and even positivized in national language and culture will be repeated within the Freudian unconscious concerning which Freud specified that it followed the logic of each national language.

Language acts as a source of recognition for oneself within the group as a non-other, as being of the group that is opposed to the foreigner/the other. In French, the noun *l'étranger* signifies both stranger and foreigner, and it is perhaps no coincidence that the term 'barbarian' (the other/the stranger) was reserved for non-Greek-language speakers in ancient Greece.

Strangeness and otherness

Yet it is not inevitable for the other to be an alien in our society. As Jacqueline Rose (2018) puts it: in the unconscious, we are not men or women, but always, and in endlessly shifting combinations, neither or both. Although there is an intrinsic violence in how the subject is constituted and how it enters the language, this is not to say that it is our inescapable predicament that the unintelligible and primitive wishes of the psyche should remain in the sphere of the repressed alien in ourselves that must be repressed, controlled and managed. Reliance on the emancipatory potential of contemplating one's own unconscious leads to acceptance of the alienation originating in the psyche. In Kristeva's words, 'henceforth, we know that we are foreigners to ourselves, and it is with the help of this sole support that we can attempt to live with others' (Kristeva, 1991, p. 170).

The aim of psychoanalysis and its methods of inquiry is about continuous probing into the unconscious in order to elucidate and bring to our conscious mind all forms of self-representation that impede our auto-gnosis (*self*-knowledge) (Fotaki, 2009b). By this, I do not mean explorations of less conscious dynamics in the crude and simplistic sense of looking into people minds to uncover their deeply hidden meanings; rather, I refer to self-reflexivity, which recognizes the process of 'othering' the fellow human, which is also universal to atrocities committed against fellow beings, including genocides. Turning to psychoanalysis in the context of political action may assist us in explicating and overcoming this divisiveness that stands in the way of our self-knowledge and impedes our autonomous thinking.

According to Cornelius Castoriadis, another post-Lacanian philosopher and psychoanalyst contemporary with Kristeva, psychoanalysis has the liberating potential to make these mutual interdependencies and relations explicit (Fotaki, 2009b). Castoriadis specifically focuses on our capacity for autonomous (from *nomos*, meaning 'law') attempts at individual and collective constitution, which is in line with Kristeva's thinking about the importance of laws as part of the symbolic:

> For it is precisely with respect to laws that foreigners *exist*. Indeed, without a social group structured about a power base and provided with legislation, that externality represented by the foreigner and most often experienced as unfavourable or at least problematical would simply not exist.
>
> (Kristeva, 1991, p. 180, italics in the original)

Concluding thoughts

Kristeva's work on abjection enables us to see the connection between the feminine/maternal body and the casting of woman in the role of the archetypal 'other', serving as a prototype for all subsequent forms of 'othering' through which separation of unwanted parts of the self occurs. This has implications for understanding why women and conceptual others are often separated from the social body. Like Irigaray and Cixous, Kristeva holds the phallogocentric nature of the symbolic responsible for excluding women because of their closeness to body and nature (Fotaki, Metcalfe, and Harding, 2014). However, like the unconscious, as Kristeva's work reminds us, the rejected body constantly threatens to return to reclaim the subject. She also offers strategies for converting abjection and exclusion into political agency. Although Butler rightly criticizes her for being insufficiently subversive (Butler, 1989), Kristeva nevertheless pioneers the use of abjection to counteract exclusion of entire groups and categories of people by reclaiming their intelligibility. Such theorization allowed for extending this to non-sanctioned sexed and gendered identities.

More importantly, Kristeva's offering of the body as a source of signification and compassion opens ways to consider different forms of otherness. Her counterpoint to primary identification based on love lies in her answer to the Lacanian symbolic, which cuts off the body and negates the importance of the maternal function, foregrounding the work of feminists who offer a concept of embodied ethics such as Bracha Ettinger (Kenny and Fotaki, 2015) and Rosi Braidotti (Fotaki and Harding, 2017, chap. 6). Although Kristeva does not directly engage with the important issue of intersectionality, her theorization on intersubjectivity (Kristeva, 1991) and 'the strangeness' of our unconscious as a root cause of various forms of exclusion holds great potential for theorizing on the dialectics of Self and Other (Braidotti, 2003, p. 45). Specifically, her psychoanalytic exploration of the otherness of the body and its links to the unconscious offers novel insights into the problems of migration, exile and otherness. Taken together, these make a unique and lasting contribution to enhancing our understanding of how subjectivities emerge through socio-symbolic processes. This is because Kristeva's entire work demonstrates that, in the end, social uses of language are not about structure, but about its function in representing our psychic and embodied lives.

Recommended reading

Original text by Kristeva

Kristeva, J. (1982). *Powers of horror: Essay on abjection*. Trans. L. Roudiez. New York, NY: Columbia University Press. (see references for further texts)

Key academic text

Oliver, K. (1993). Julia Kristeva's feminist revolutions. *Hypatia*, 8(3), pp. 95–116 (on Kristeva's contributions to feminist thought on the body).

Accessible resource

Fotaki, M. (2017). *TEDx turning fear to purpose*. Available at: www.youtube.com/watch?v=-aP_Ug11La4 (on othering of the refugees and on overcoming the fear of the other).

References

Baxter, J. (2003). *Positioning gender in discourse: A feminist methodology*. New York, NY: Springer.

Braidotti, R. (2003). Becoming woman: Or sexual difference revisited. *Theory, Culture & Society*, 20(3), pp. 43–64.

Butler, J. (1989). The body politics of Julia Kristeva. *Hypatia*, 3(3), pp. 104–118.

Butler, J. (1993). *Bodies that matter: On the discursive limits of 'Sex'*. London: Verso.

Butler, J. (1997). *The psychic life of power: Theories in subjection*. London: Routledge.

Butler, J. (2004). *Precarious lives: The powers of mourning and violence*. London: Verso.

Douglas, M. (1966). *Purity and danger: An analysis of concepts of pollution and taboo*. London: Routledge.

Edelstein, M. (1992). Metaphor, meta-narrative, and mater-narrative in Kristeva's 'Stabat Mater'. In: D. Crownfield, ed., *Body/text in Julia Kristeva: Religion, women, and psychoanalysis*. New York, NY: SUNY Press, pp. 27–52.

Fotaki, M. (2009a). The unwanted body of man or why is it so difficult for women to make it in academe? A feminist psychoanalytic approach. In: M. Özbilgin, ed., *Equality, diversity and inclusion at work: A research companion*. Cheltenham: Edward Elgar Press, pp. 157–171.

Fotaki, M. (2009b) 'The ghosts of the past, the dreamlands of the future . . .' *Journal of Communist and Post-Communist Studies*. Special Issue: *The Ghosts of the Past: 20th Anniversary of the Fall of Communism in Europe and Russia*, 42, pp. 217–232.

Fotaki, M. (2011). The sublime object of desire (for knowledge): Sexuality at work in business and management schools in England. *British Journal of Management*, 22(1), pp. 42–53.

Fotaki, M. (2012). Woman's absence from the body of knowledge: The experience of female lecturers in business and management schools in England. In: F. Festic, ed., *Gender and trauma*. Cambridge: Cambridge Scholars, pp. 191–214.

Fotaki, M. (2013). No woman is like a man (in academia): The masculine symbolic order and the unwanted female body. *Organization Studies*, 34(9), pp. 1251–1275.

Fotaki, M. and Harding, N. (2013). Lacan and sexual difference in organization and management theory: Towards a hysterical academy? *Organization*, 20(2), pp. 153–172.

Fotaki, M. and Harding, N. (2017). *Gender and the organization. Women at work in the 21st century*. London: Routledge.

Fotaki, M., Metcalfe, B. and Harding, N. (2014). Writing materiality into organization theory. *Human Relations*, 67(10), pp. 1239–1263.

Freud, S. (2003 [1919]). *The uncanny*. Trans. D. McLintock. London: Penguin.

Gambaudo, S. (2017). Is there such a thing as 'woman writing'? *Angelaki*, 22(10), pp. 23–33.

Gatrell, C. (2017). Boundary creatures? Employed, breastfeeding mothers and 'abjection as practice'. *Organization Studies*. doi:10.1177/0170840617736932

Höpfl, H. (2000). The suffering mother and the miserable son: Organizing women and organizing women's writing. *Gender, Work and Organization*, 17(2), pp. 98–105.

Hunter, C. and Kivinen, N. (2017). Constructing girlhood: Abject labour in magazine offices. *Gender, Work and Organization*, 24(6), pp. 566–581.

Jonte-Pace, D. (1992). Situating Kristeva differently: Psychoanalytic reading of women and religion. In: D. Crownfield, ed., *Body/text in Julia Kristeva: Religion, women, and psychoanalysis*. New York, NY: SUNY Press, pp. 1–22.

Kenny, K. (2010). Beyond ourselves: Passion and the dark side of identification in an ethical organization. *Human Relations*, 63(6), pp. 857–873.

Kenny, K. (2012). 'Someone big and important': Identification and affect in an international development organization. *Organization Studies*, 33(9), pp. 1175–1193.

Kenny, K. (2016). Organizations and violence: The child as abject-boundary in Ireland's industrial schools. *Organization Studies*, 37(7), pp. 939–961.

Kenny, K. and Fotaki, M. (2015). From gendered organizations to compassionate borderspaces: Reading corporeal ethics with Bracha Ettinger. *Organization*, 22(2), pp. 183–199.

Kristeva, J. (1969). *Sémiotikè: Recherches Pour Une Sémanalyse*. Paris: Seuil.

Kristeva, J. (1977). *Polylogue*, Paris: Seuil.

Kristeva, J. (1980). *Desire in language*. Ed. L. Roudiez, Trans. T. Gora, A. Jardine, and L. Roudiez. New York, NY: Columbia University Press.

Kristeva, J. (1986). Revolution in poetic language. Trans. M. Waller. In: T. Moi, ed., *The Kristeva reader*. Oxford: Blackwell, pp. 89–136.

Kristeva, J. (1987). *In the beginning was love: Psychoanalysis and faith*. New York, NY: Columbia University Press.

Kristeva, J. (1989). *Black sun: Depression and melancholia*. Trans. L. S. Roudiez. New York, NY: Columbia University Press.

Kristeva, J. (1991). *Strangers to ourselves*. Trans. L. S. Roudiez. New York, NY: Columbia University Press.

Kristeva, J. (1998). The subject in process. In: P. Ffrench, and R. F. Lack, eds., *The tel quel reader*. New York, NY: Routledge, pp. 133–178.

Kristeva, J. (2004). *Kristeva Holberg lecture. Thinking about liberty in the dark times*. Available at: www.holbergprisen.no/en/holberg-lecture-2004-thinking-about-liberty-dark-times

Moi, T. (1988). *Sexual/textual politics: Feminist literary theory*. London: Routledge.

Phillips, M. and Rippin, A. (2010). Howard and the mermaid: Abjection and the Starbucks' foundation memoir. *Organization*, 17(4), pp. 481–499.

Phillips, R. (2014). Abjection. *Transgender Studies Quarterly*, 1(1–2), pp. 19–21.

Rizq, R. (2013). States of abjection. *Organization Studies*, 34(9), pp. 1277–1297.

Rose, J. (2018). I am a knife. *London Review of Books*, 40(4), 22 February. Available at: www.lrb.co.uk/v40/n04/jacqueline-rose/i-am-a-knife.

Sørensen, B. M. (2014). Changing the memory of suffering: An organizational aesthetics of the dark side. *Organization Studies*, 35(2), pp. 279–302.

Tyler, I. (2009). Against abjection. *Feminist theory*, 10(1), pp. 77–98.

Tyler, M. (2011). Tainted love: From dirty work to abject labour in Soho's sex shops. *Human Relations*, 64(11), pp. 1477–1500.

5 Marguerite Yourcenar

Anticipating the (queer) body (in organization studies)

Chris Steyaert

To nominate the literary work of the French novelist and essayist Marguerite Yourcenar (1903–1987) for its significant potential to contribute to the understanding of organization might come to most as a surprise or even far-fetched. As there is no direct translation from literature to organization (Pick, 2017), it does not suffice to read and appreciate Yourcenar's fascinating novels to reap intriguing insights on organization. Instead, what we can argue with the philosopher Gilles Deleuze is that in literature we arrive at the importance of what is not said (Alesch, 2007): 'A work of art is worth more than a philosophical work; for what is enveloped in the sign is more profound than all the explicit significations' (Deleuze, 2000, p. 30). These silences are also in focus for Yourcenar, who thought that 'literary texts distinguish themselves from other written items by incorporating *open, or silent areas* which enable them to surpass what would otherwise be no more than an agglomeration of signs' (Alesch, 2007, p. 28; my italics). This chapter is inspired by Yourcenar: 'The written word has taught me to listen to the human voice, much as the great unchanging statues have taught me to appreciate bodily motions. On the other hand, but more slowly, life has thrown light for me on the meaning of books' (Yourcenar, 2000).

This then becomes the premise of this chapter: through reading and interpreting (some of) the literary work of Marguerite Yourcenar, we might point at silences in organization studies, and speak about those things we cannot (easily) speak about. Through literature, we might regain our alertness to consider carefully the interplay between what is concealed and revealed in studies of organization. This should not be so difficult: there are many topics and concepts that organization studies is rather unconcerned or careless about, which get full if not explicit attention in Yourcenar's writings. For instance, the work of Yourcenar is not insignificant for understanding the body and its related themes of sexuality, desire and love. These can hardly be called the favourite topics of organization studies: its ways of producing knowledge have seldom been confronted with an epistemology of the closet (Sedgwick, 1990) and the latter's willingness to question these 'omissions' as strategic silences (Hekanaho, 2007).

Even then, these notions are not stand-alone thoughts but are interlinked with organizational issues of freedom, power and ethics. We can already point out that Yourcenar's most important novel, *Memoirs of Hadrian*, is about the Roman emperor Hadrian, which gives us a view on leadership that comes with a problematization of masculinist heteronormativity (Miller, 2012). Also the smaller circles that explore queer approaches to organization (Pullen et al., 2016) might find Yourcenar's work revealing. Even if Yourcenar's work has sometimes been criticized for its lack of contribution to (specific forms of) feminist causes (Cliche, 2004),[1] current re-readings of her novels are seeing them as anticipating and illustrative of certain ways in which queer theory unfolds (Hekanaho, 2006; 2007). Therefore, these reviews of how Yourcenar has been received 'belie the more common picture of her as a classical stylist, scholar, and aesthete, and reveal her to be an engaged writer, perhaps not in the mode of [de] Beauvoir, but nonetheless in surprising and significant ways' (Miller, 2012, p. 264).

In particular, Marguerite Yourcenar belongs to a group of female literates that have reframed life through anti-normative fluidity and multiplicity (Hynynen, 2010) following a Heraclitean view on time.[2] Yourcenar has realized this emphasis on (sexual) fluidity by exploring the lives of a series of original 'personages' in historical novels that range from Roman and Greek antiquity, over Flanders in early Renaissance, south Italy in the seventeenth century, to the Baltic after the Great War. In this variety of times and sites, she mainly zoomed in on homo- (or bi-)sexual protagonists in some of her best-known novels such as *Alexis, Memoirs of Hadrian* and *The Abyss* (Yourcenar, 1981a). But she has also re-counted the lives of (classical) women (Braund, 2012; Poniewaz, 2013), as in the early novel *Anna, soror* (Yourcenar, 1991) or in her bundle of poetic essays, *Fires* (Yourcenar, 1981c). In that sense, we have to read her novels which – long before there was ever talk of queer theory – question normative heterosexuality so that we can alter our capacity to see different possibilities of sexuality and freedom. And, if all that is not enough, Marguerite Yourcenar – autodidact, nonconformist and anachronistic – learned a thing or two about gendered institutional life as she crossed the more than 300-year-old gender boundary by becoming the first woman ever to join the French Academy.[3] Let us turn now to that controversial scene where in 1981, Yourcenar – under the sounds of drumroll – entered the male bastion of French academic organization.

Entering the Académie Française

Marguerite Yourcenar was elected to the French Academy on March 6, 1980, only with one vote more than needed. This result reflected that many members of the Academy – among others Claude Lévi-Strauss – were squarely against a woman entering their select club of 'immortels' – the seal 'à l'immortalité' was given as, once elected, you became a lifelong member (Sarnecki and O'Sickey, 2004). At that historic moment on January 22, 1981, when Yourcenar was about to begin her 'discours de réception' under the 'Coupule' at Quai Conti in the presence of the then French president Giscard d'Estaing and his wife, Yourcenar had obtained back her French nationality. At the dawn of World War II, Marguerite Yourcenar had been writing in South Italy on her novel *Le coup de grâce*, a story about a triangle relationship set in the Baltics during the Russian civil war (Yourcenar, 1981b). This short novel – with a strong autobiographical reference[4] – tells about a woman who is rejected by an aristocrat as he had eyes for her brother. Afterwards, Yourcenar travelled through Austria and Germany, witnessing an increasing war climate instigated by the violent uprising of Nazism. In search of a job, she felt she needed to return to France, but there was nobody there who could help her. At that moment, Grace Frick (whom she had met previously by accident in a Parisian hotel) invited Marguerite to join her. Yourcenar decided to accept the invitation and move to the United States, travelling in November 1939 to New York for an initial six months. The war broke out, and Yourcenar continued to live in America with Grace Frick for 40 years until the latter's death in November 1979 following a long illness (Howard, 2018).

Later, in her conversations with Matthieu Galey (1984b), Yourcenar said that she belongs to everyone, as she is not eager to identify with a particular background or nation. Born in Brussels from a Franco-Belgian family, Yourcenar[5] will not only keep her relations warm with Flanders or France, but she will travel across Europe and the world, especially being intensively involved with the East. Paradoxically, Yourcenar will alternate this nomadic life with long periods of isolation when she lives with (the increasingly ill) Grace Frick on Mount Desert Island off the coast to Maine in a house that they called 'Petite Plaisance', or little pleasure. When the news of her election reached Yourcenar just a few months after Grace had passed away, she was already travelling, something she has done her whole life and picked up again with a gay, younger friend Jerry Wilson – her own Antinous.

In 1988, their house became a museum, giving insight in the life world of two women – their travel paraphernalia, photos and books – living together long before the sexual revolution and gay and lesbian emancipation of the late '60s occurred (Howard, 2018): 'In the study, there is a large custom-made table with two typewriters opposite each other. As Yourcenar wrote her novels, and Frick translated them, they sat face to face, a few feet apart'.[6] In this world of writing and translating,

the most striking feature of the house is the library, which stretches
from floor to ceiling and from room to room: Asian literature in the
parlour, Greek and Roman in the study, seventeenth and eighteenth
century in the foyer, early nineteenth century in Frick's bedroom, later
nineteenth century in the guest rooms, twentieth century in Yourcenar's
room. The place looks like the Bibliothèque Nationale crammed into a
New England farmhouse,[7]

The different literatures refer to the various historical periods in which
Yourcenar placed her novels. It shows her life as scholar and booklover,
someone who wrote 'with an almost eerie accuracy'[8] and prepared her novels meticulously, noticeable also in the many erudite prefaces or detailed
postscripts that accompany her fiction.[9]

Today, few people are aware that Yourcenar became the first woman to
be inducted in the French Academy. Just the fact that Yourcenar was proposed can be seen as a surprise as she had not participated for so long in the
intellectual life in Paris. However, the significance of breaking through a
350-year-old barrier cannot be underestimated, noted as it was in the head-
lines of papers and television worldwide. The next day, the *New York Times*
opened its report as follows: 'A procession of immortality, looking extraor-
dinarily mortal with its white hair and stiff backs, cautiously descended the
main staircase of the Académie Française this afternoon. In its midst, for the
first time in 346 years, was a woman'. Whatever position one took on this
controversial election, Yourcenar stood up to the occasion, as she spoke the
opening remarks of her acceptance speech, paying tribute to all women who
could have gone before her:

> You have welcomed me, as I was saying. This uncertain, floating self, this
> entity whose existence I myself have contested, which I only feel to be
> truly delimited by the several works that I have happened to write, here
> it is, such as it is, surrounded and accompanied by an invisible troupe of
> women who should, perhaps, have received this honor much earlier, to
> the point where I am tempted to step back to let their shadows pass.

Yourcenar took the chair of Roger Caillois, more precisely chair three of the
40 chairs the French Academy counts. With these words, the Academy must
have realized in the first minutes of this ceremony that they had elected a
new member who would not deliver a speech as one can expect and antici-
pate. In any case, before Yourcenar had refused to go begging for votes
and had said she would not move to France to assist the weekly Thursday
meeting. At the same time, she had suggested that if these men were ready
to accept a woman among them for the first time, she would never be so

impolite to France to refuse this honour. However, she had declined to dress in the 'uniform' of the Academy, let alone to carry and lift their sword. Instead, the 77-year-old woman was wearing a black dress designed by Yves St. Laurent with a white collar and a white silk scarf.

Yourcenar, called the nomad of the French Academy (Savigneau, 1993), thus began her oration 'by radically undermining the logocentric notion of a unitary self' (Sarnecki and O'Sickey, 2004, p. 14), a deconstruction of the metaphysics of identity in front of her 'big ego' male colleagues present. Instead, she inserted herself 'in a women writers' genealogy' (p. 15), as she continued to sum up the women who the Academy could have easily elected before her:

> Madame de Staël would no doubt have been ineligible by virtue of her Swiss ancestry and her Swedish marriage: she contented herself with being one of the best minds of the century. George Sand would have caused a scandal because of her turbulent life, because of the very generosity of her emotions, which made her such an admirably womanly woman; the person even more so than the writer was ahead of her time. Colette herself thought that it was not for a woman to go calling on men soliciting their votes, and I can only agree, not having done so myself.

Sarnecki and O'Sickey (2004, p. 15) note the 'enormous importance' of how Yourcenar positions herself, finally admitting what beforehand she had denied, 'that being a woman was a political matter, having to do with the positionality, with the space where one found oneself'. In referring to her books as something that happened, Yourcenar does not set up herself as the guiding force of her writings, and distances herself from the male metaphors in favour of female ones to speak of the writing process (Taat, 2004).[10] Instead, writing consists of the slow and difficult task to let the voices of characters emerge beyond the ego and narcissism of the author (Taat, 2004). This is exemplified in the voices of Alexis and Hadrian, from two novels written as (long) letters, belonging respectively to her early and later work.

Alexis: a coming out epistolary *avant la lettre*

If Yourcenar's entry at the French Academy came with a paradigm-shifting break with tradition (Ambrecht, 2007), the 'real' change comes with her understanding of sexuality, subjectivity and the body. Alexis – which Yourcenar published at the age of 26 – is a short novel with the subtitle *Ou le traité du vain combat*, announcing that the struggle of Alexis will be in vain (Yourcenar, 1984a). In this early work, the love between men sets the stage for a long series of gay love relationships to follow. For instance, between Eric and Conrad in *Le coup de grâce* but also between Hadrian and Antinous (see below), where 'she played a masterful trump card, situating her characters in a time and place that valued love relationships between men' (Alesch, 2007, p. 11). Against the zeitgeist, Yourcenar refused to consider same-sex relationships as problematic; on the contrary, people always get better through their love, both emotionally and morally (Alesch, 2007). Alexis as transgressive protagonist is 'both innocent and profoundly moral' (Ibid., p. 10), not least by the conscientious way through which he addresses his wife in this letter in an attempt to (make her) understand and eventually accept his feelings for men. In the preface to the English edition, Yourcenar remains convinced that the drama between Alexis and Monique would repeat itself as long as society sets up such corrupt prohibitions, destroying pure hearts, not least through language and the obstacles it can infuse:

> It has perhaps not been adequately observed that the problem of sexual freedom in all its forms is, in large part, a problem of freedom of expression. It seems clear that, from generation to generation, the tendencies and the acts themselves vary little; on the contrary what changes is the extent of the zone of silence or the weight of the layers of lies surrounding them.
>
> (p. ix)

Even if homosexuality was an audacious theme in the late 1920s, Yourcenar approaches transgressive sexuality and love with sympathy (Hynynen, 2011). With Alexis's story, difficult emotions – how forbidden love is experienced and slowly can become accepted – are mediated by how we can speak about it:

> Yet there is something absurd in shrouding with phrases a confession that should be simple: I would laugh at that, if only I could laugh. It is humiliating to think that so many chaotic hopes, emotions, and troubles (not counting all the suffering) have a physiological reason. That thought first made me ashamed before it calmed me.
>
> (p. 16)

Alexis goes back and forth between feelings of humiliation, pain, bitterness and sadness. He is consternated that any desire that comes from the body would not be an acceptable and accepted feeling.

In Alexis's struggle, silence and feeling silenced forms a rhythm that colours his life. As a child, Alexis grows up in only female company and experiences the tranquillity and peacefulness that radiates from his mother and sisters (Hynynen, 2010): 'My infancy was silent and solitary; it left me shy and consequently taciturn' (p. 12). However, silence refers also to the inhibitions and taboos that Alexis experiences. He will never be able to admit to his mother before she dies that he likes men: 'It felt as though a confession was going to pour out of me, involuntarily, like tears' (p. 45), but as a maid comes in and the moment passes, he spared himself 'an irreparable, pointless error' (p. 46). Instead Alexis will marry, adding pressure to himself, until he can no longer stand his own secrecy and silence:

> When I think that I have known you for more than three years and that it is only now I dare speak to you for the first time! And even now it is only by letter, and only because I must. It is awful that silence can be such a fault; it is the worst of my faults, but I have committed it. Long before I committed it against you, I committed it against myself. Once silence has established itself in a house, it is hard to get it out; the more important a matter is, the more it seems one wants to keep it silent.
>
> (pp. 12–13)

During several years of 'struggle, obsession and severity' (p. 49), Alexis tries everything: first isolation: 'The first consequence of forbidden inclinations is to wall us up within ourselves' (p. 42); then control: 'I remember that I believed I could methodically arrange my desires and anguishes, the way one arranges objects in a drawer' (p. 48); and even abstention: 'I condemned myself, at the age of twenty, to an absolute isolation of the senses and the heart' (p. 49). And, with it, a palette of unhappy affects comes: agony – 'I had moments of agony when I thought I would die' (p. 43); loneliness – 'one struggles in solitude as if at the center of a crystal' (p. 43); and confusion – 'I found it admirable to renounce what, several months earlier, I believed I was horrified by' (p. 49). At some point, the struggle is so strong that Alexis increasingly thinks of death and dying: 'In Vienna, during those years of inner conflict, I often hoped to die' (p. 60).

However, music can bring some solace. Alexis, as musician, stops playing, once he has married and the layers of lies widen, extending the zone of silence around him:

> I had completely abandoned music. Music was a part of the world in which I was resigned never to live again. They say that music is the realm of the soul; that may be, my dear: it simply proves that soul and flesh are not separable, that one contains the other, the way a keyboard contains sounds. The silence which follows music is not at all like ordinary silences: it is a heedful silence; it is a living silence.
>
> (p. 89)

When he later starts to play again, he feels very strongly about the effects of his inner struggle: 'It was hate: hate for everything that had falsified me and crushed me for so long' (p. 102). Indeed, Yourcenar, who affirms desire through its connection with and the primacy of the body, is discrete with regard to describing sexual acts and uses his hands as primary erotic zones (Hynynen, 2010). His hands, which Alexis calls his only friends, refer to his tactile sensuality, the hands he uses to play piano as well as to caress men's bodies: 'my hands, placed before me on the keys, troubled me with the memory of caresses' (p. 62).

In this way, his erotic desires align with his love for music. His ability to turn around his sexual suppression falls together with regaining his power to play piano. Looking at his hands, Alexis says, 'it was as if I saw my soul before my eyes, twice alive' (p. 102). Indeed, any struggle to fight against desires of the body is in vain, and his struggle to come to terms with his desires is through appreciating his hands, his body:

> in them were contained all future deeds, just as all possible sounds sleep within the piano. They had encircled bodies in the brief joy of embraces; they had touched, on resonant keyboards, the form of invisible notes; they had, in the dark, traced with a caress the contours of sleeping bodies. . . . They were etiolated, as pale as the ivory on which they rested, for I had deprived them of sunshine, or of work, and of joy.
>
> (pp. 102–103)

In the end, Alexis abandons his struggle and accepts when he says he prefers 'a sin (if that is what it is) to a denial of self which leads to self-destruction'. Even if Alexis believes his sexuality resembles somehow a prison of desiring, he goes on to accept himself. After all, acceptance should not be difficult if all of us, indeed the whole of society, does the same:

> That day I had, by means of my entire body, which was astonished to live again, my second revelation of the beauty of the world. You know what the first one was. As I did at the first one, I wept, not so much from happiness or from gratitude; I wept at the idea that life was so simple and would be so easy if we ourselves were only simple enough to accept it.
>
> (pp. 67–68)

Indeed, living needs the art of music and the silence it brings: not a silence to forget the web of lies spun around one's self, but one that brings us closer to the sound of the mysteries of living which Alexis hears in how the flowing water produces a sound in a fountain: 'it has always seemed to me that music ought to be nothing but the overflowing of a great silence' (p. 64). The silence of self-acceptance and happiness.

With this coming out story *avant la lettre*, Yourcenar anticipates here an ethical-aesthetic version of what Eve Kosofsky Sedgwick (1990) later calls 'an epistemology of the closet'. Alexis's letter shows well the impossibility of coming out of the closet, and its paradoxical stance as an 'open secret' (Sedgwick, 1990). As Alexis 'muses on the shifting boundaries of truth and lie, secrecy and openness, or narration, confession, and silence' (Hekanaho, 2007, p. 89), Yourcenar illustrates the discursive structure of the closet, and both of them simultaneously construct and deconstruct the closet as an area of unarticulated sexual secret. For Sedgwick, this area is not just relevant for the identity formation of individual people, but more generally refers to Western culture and its cultural politics of knowledge, as she claims that 'an understanding of virtually any aspect of substance must be, not merely incomplete, but damaged in its central substance to the degree that it does not incorporate a critical analysis of modern homo/heterosexual definition' (p. 1). Alexis's letter illustrates well that 'the unarticulated knowledge identified by the closet is produced and regulated by the strategic silences and rhetoric of circumvention, coded expressions, and omissions' (Hekanaho, 2007, p. 90). In that sense, the closet is less about the discussion of sexual secrets but it offers a methodology to investigate the production of knowledge more generally. Therefore, reading this novel on coming out with the eyes of Sedgwick projects Yourcenar's focus on male homosexuality onto 'a larger discussion on cultural silences, silencing acts, and the ways and rights of representation of the different, dissident, aberrant, or queer positions of knowing and producing knowledge' (Hekanaho, 2007, p. 90). In Sedgwick's view, secrecy/disclosure and private/public form epistemologically charged pairings, condensed in the figures of 'the closet' and 'coming out'; they have marked other pairings 'as basic to modern cultural organization as masculine/feminine, majority/minority, innocence/initiation, natural/artificial, new/old, growth/decadence, urbane/provincial, health/illness, same/different, cognition/paranoia, art/kitsch, sincerity/sentimentality, and voluntarily/addiction' (Sedgwick, 1990, p. 72). The eccentric position that comes with the closet enables a queer view to critique and analyze organizational discourses not informed by mainstream structures of knowledge (McDonald, 2016) but by reading and decoding the 'open secrets' of organizational life and by making visible 'alternative, queer locations of knowledge and competence in interpretation' (Hekanaho, 2007, p. 92). For instance, Pia Hekanaho takes Yourcenar's oeuvre not in the first place as representing homosexuality but as an illustration of (textual) female masculinity (Halberstam, 1998), which allows her also to explain 'the conflicting critical reception of Yourcenar's writing, and the queer textuality pervading her work' (p. 93).

Sexuality, freedom and power in *Memoirs of Hadrian*

This novel, which was called in a review of the *Spectator* 'an enthralling meditation on power, politics, love and death' (Salisbury, 2005) is also written as a (very long) letter, this time from Hadrian to his potential successor and later emperor – his adopted son Marcus Aurelius – to reflect upon his life now that he begins to discern the profile of his death and to instruct his successor to rule wisely:

> Little by little this letter, begun in order to tell you of the progress of my illness, has become the diversion of a man who no longer has the energy required for continued application to affairs of state; it has become, in fact, the written meditation of a sick man who holds audience with his memories. I propose now to do more than this: I have formed a project for telling you about my life.
>
> (Yourcenar, 2000, p. 28)

In this 'portrait of a voice', Yourcenar lets an emperor speak, a man 'who was almost wise' (p. 274) and who, as a leader, tried to make a difference through his pacifist stance and his inclination for Hellenic values. Nicknamed 'little Greek', Hadrian aspired to rule well (Groppa, 2017) and to pacify and stabilize the empire (Heynders, 2013). With choosing someone from such a distant time and world, the book brings 'an undisputed appeal to the restoration of the ethical-political bases of a world devastated by World War II' (Groppa, 2017, p. 314).

Furthermore, Hadrian shows self-reflection and self-relativism (Heynders, 2013) about his life and leadership which is seen as a form of serving. Yourcenar brings a gendered understanding of leadership, with a 'preference for a critical, self-reflecting and serving leader, combining principles and pragmatism' (Heynders, 2013, p. 82). Even if Hadrian's ethical-political interpretation of his role as leader and his extreme self-reflexivity on this role are striking, even more surprising is the way his life and leadership are defined through the themes of the body, sexuality and love. For instance, in the opening of the book, he reflects on health, on mediation and on sound sleeping (Heynders, 2013). Having just visited his doctor, the book opens with Hadrian saying:

> This morning it occurred to me for the first time that my body, my faithful companion and friend, truer and better known to me than my own soul, may be after all only a sly beast who will end by devouring his

master. But enough. . . . I like my body; it has served me well, and in every way, and I do not begrudge it the care it now needs.

(p. 15)

His life and leadership is presented as being primarily embodied, making him wonder a little later: 'Alas, why does my mind, even in its best days, never possess but a particle of the assimilative powers of the body?' (p. 19). Although this novel has been analyzed extensively within the tradition of French modernist literature, more recently the novel is recognized for the way it illustrates a position on freedom that anticipates the later arguments of Michel Foucault on freedom and power, which relativize the construction of the modern normative subject (Miller, 2012). In particular, both their concept of freedom is understood 'as a set of practices exercised by the self on itself, which is derived from the ancient traditions of Stoic and Socratic philosophy' and is 'firmly implicated in a simultaneous problematization of masculinist heteronormativity and the erotic' (p. 264). At some point, Hadrian writes:

For my part I have sought liberty more than power, and power only because it can lead to freedom. What interested me was not a philosophy of the free man (all who try that have proved tiresome), but a technique: I hoped to discover the hinge where our will meets and moves with destiny, and where discipline strengthens, instead of restraining, our nature. Understanding clearly that there is no question of harsh Stoic will. . . . No, I have dreamed of a more secret acquiescence, or of a more supple response. Life was to me a horse to whose motion one yields, but only after having trained the animal to the utmost. Since everything is finally a decision of the mind, however slowly and imperceptible made, and involves also the body's assent, I strove to attain by degrees to that state of liberty, or of submission, which is almost pure.

(pp. 47–48)

It is the engagement of the body – and the exercises of care and submission it enacts – that remind us of freedom as a set of practices in Foucault's ethics of the care of the self (Steyaert, 2010). Hadrian in referring to practices, techniques and disciplines uses the very terms that Foucault (1990; 1995) used to formulate his ethical turn in the *History of Sexuality*. Also ethical leadership is a practice that allows, based on a momentary slackening of the reins, 'a certain space of nondetermination, which permits the subject in turn to master itself' (Miller, 2012, p. 274). At this point, as Paul Miller (2012) notes, we hear a prophetic voice that turns itself against the alienation of modern industrial society as well as the over-identification of late capitalism, when Hadrian imagines a form of servitude that aims to avoid 'in transforming men into stupid and satisfied machines, who believe themselves free when they are enslaved, or by developing in them a taste for work as fanatical as the passion for war among the barbarian races'.[11]

Instead, Yourcenar uses the history of Hadrian to turn to his love story with Antinous that forms the apex of the novel in a part called 'the golden era'. This love that ended abruptly with Antinous's drowning in the Nile forms an incisive experience for Hadrian that allows him to reconsider his past as emperor and as human being. As Hadrian reflects upon his life, he realizes that the memories of his lost love touch him much more than his achievements as leader:

> In such an evaluation, certain works of short duration are surely negligible; yet occupations which have been extended over a whole lifetime signify just as little. For example, it seems to me as I write this hardly important to have been emperor.
>
> (p. 32)

Hadrian speaks bluntly about his love for another man: same-sex attraction goes without saying, something which was exactly the opposite at the time when Yourcenar was writing and long hereafter. However, 'the position from which Yourcenar addressed sexual preference and the gendering of power in the Mémoires was not that of a political polemic' (Miller, 2012, p. 278). Instead, Hadrian says:

> I have sometimes thought of constructing a system of human knowledge which would be based on eroticism, a theory of contact, wherein the mysterious value of each being is to offer to us just that point of perspective which another world affords. In such a philosophy pleasure would be a more complete, but also a more specialized form of approach to the Other, one more technique for getting to know what is not ourselves.
>
> (Yourcenar, p. 24)

Of course, the format of a letter enacts this idea of a philosophy of contact, as Hadrian tries to convince Marcus Aurelius, who has been in isolation from his contact with the world, that his life and leadership mostly evolved through his relationships with other, with what is not him, most of all, his lover Antinous. It is embodied love that gives us access to another world, and to happiness:

> My life in which everything arrived late, power, happiness too, acquired the splendor of midday, filled with sunlight like the hours of the siesta

when everything bathes in an atmosphere of gold, the objects in the bedroom and the body stretched out along our side.[12]

Conclusion

This series is about bringing women back to the spotlight on a stage that has only zoomed in on male figures. With bringing Yourcenar (back) on the scene, we notice how she herself reminded the male community of the French Academy of the women they could have inducted in the last 100 years or so. More importantly, Yourcenar anticipates proto-Foucauldian understandings of power and freedom that informed poststructuralist reframings in organization studies. Yourcenar's writings uncover important silences as they give voice to stories of men and women that live their lives outside heterosexual expectations and as they increase our capacity to see what sexual freedom and political agency could be. Her writing follows an epistemology of the body and the erotic that affirms how desire partakes in the gestation of living and loving, but also leading and labour. Seeing in statues the possibility of movement, Yourcenar's writing aims to give to those frozen historical documents the suppleness and warmth of living things and the fluidity of lived life (Taat, 1986, p. 61). Reminiscent of Monique Wittig's idea in the *Lesbian Body* (1975, p. 10), expressing 'the desire to give intense life to the real body in the words of the book',[13] we find here a queer tactic to re-think the relationship between writing, sexuality and embodied life (Ambrecht, 2007). If there is a possibility to queer the discipline of organization studies, returning to the writings of Marguerite Yourcenar and the way she underlines the body and anticipates the queer body, remains an unexpected but promising option, for sure:

> What perhaps makes sensual pleasure so terrible is that it teaches us we have a body. . . . This body, which appears so fragile, is nonetheless more durable than my virtuous resolutions, perhaps even more durable than my soul, for often the soul dies in advance of the body.
>
> (Alexis, p. 45)

Notes

1 This assessment remains complex, even if Yourcenar's style as a feminine writing is increasingly underlined; see Southwood (2013) and Taat (1986; 2004).
2 Virginia Woolf comes to mind (Steyaert, 2015). Yourcenar to her delight met Woolf as she translated *The Waves*, and wanted to clarify some questions she had with regard to this novel.
3 Notice that Yourcenar was already nominated in 1971 to the Royal Belgian Academy as a foreign member. She was also one of the first women to receive the prestigious Erasmus prize in the Netherlands.

4 In this case, Yourcenar was said to struggle with her unrequited passion for her publisher, André Fraigneau. Her novels are seen as 'testimonials of tremendous and undying passion' (Alesch, 2007, p. 4).
5 Yourcenar is a reduced anagram of her real name, de Crayencour.
6 Quoted in the *New Yorker* of February 14, 2005: 'Becoming the emperor. How Marguerite Yourcenar reinvented the past'.
7 Ibid.
8 Ibid.
9 See also Alesch, 2007. For instance, Yourcenar consulted 17 pages of resources to write the *Memoirs of Hadrian*.
10 Such as gestation, fertility or Mother Earth, see also Taat (1986).
11 Translated by and quoted in Miller (2012, p. 274).
12 Ibid., p. 280.
13 Quoted in Southwood (2013, p. 196).

Recommended reading

Original text by Yourcenar

Yourcenar, M. (1984). *Alexis. A novel*. New York, NY: Farrar, Straus and Giroux.

Key academic text

Miller, P. A. (2012). Hadrian's practice of freedom: Yourcenar, Beauvoir, and Foucault. *Eugesta*, 2, pp. 263–286.

Accessible resource

Yourcenar, M. (2000). *Memoirs of Hadrian*. London: Penguin Books.

References

Alesch, S. J. (2007). *Marguerite Yourcenar: The other/reader*. Birmingham: Summa Publications.
Ambrecht, T.J.D. (2007). *At the periphery of the center: Sexuality and literary genre in the works of Marguerite Yourcenar and Julien Green*. Amsterdam: Editions Rodopi.
Braund, S. (2012). We're her too, the ones without names. A study of female voices as imagined by Margaret Atwood, Carol Ann Duffy, and Marguerite Yourcenar. *Classical Receptions Journal*, 4(2), pp. 190–218.
Cliche, E. (2004). Performing the masculine voice. In: J. H. Sarnecki, and I. M. O'Sickey, eds., *Subversive subjects: Reading Marguerite Yourcenar*. Madison: Farleigh Dickinson University Press, pp. 77–100.
Deleuze, G. (2000/1964) *Proust and signs*. London: The Athlone Press.
Foucault, M. (1990). *History of sexuality*. Vol. 2. New York, NY: Vintage Books.
Foucault, M. (1995). *History of sexuality*. Vol. 3. New York, NY: Vintage Books.

Groppa, A. J. (2017). Dialogues in delay: Speculations about a whole other temporality of the pedagogical encounter. *Educ. Pesqui*, 43(2), pp. 311–327.

Halberstam, J. (1998). *Female masculinity*. Durham: Duke University Press.

Hekanaho, P. L. (2006). A kind of bitter longing: Masculine bodies and textual female masculinity in *Brokeback Mountain* and *Memoirs of Hadrian*. *SQS*, 02, pp. 4–21.

Hekanaho, P. L. (2007). Speaking out from the closet? The queer reader's position of knowledge and the works of Marguerite Yourcenar. *SQS*, 01, pp. 89–94.

Heynders, O. (2013). Great men. Political leadership in literature. *Tijdschrift Voor Nederlandse Taal & Letterkunde*, 129(1), pp. 69–83.

Howard, J. E. (2018). *We met in Paris. Grace Frick and her life with Marguerite Yourcenar*. Missouri, Columbia: University of Missouri Press.

Hynynen, A. (2010). Pluralite et fluidité antinormatives. *Etudes sur les transgressions sexuelles dans l'oeuvre de Marguerite Yourcenar*. Abo: Abo University Press.

Hynynen, A. (2011). Le chercheur queer et le roman historique: Quelques défis de Marguerite Yourcenar. *Itinéraires*, 1, pp. 137–154.

McDonald, J. (2016). Expanding queer reflexivity: The closet as a guiding metaphor for reflexive practice. *Management Learning*, 47(4), pp. 391–406.

Miller, P. A. (2012). Hadrian's practice of freedom: Yourcenar, Beauvoir, and Foucault. *Eugesta*, 2, pp. 263–286.

Pick, D. (2017). Rethinking organization theory: The fold, the rhizome and the seam between organization and the literary. *Organization*, 24(6), pp. 800–818.

Poniewaz, K. A. (2013). Alcestes and her sisters: Feminism, sorority and tragedy in Yourcenar and Simones Alcestes. *Women in French Studies*, 21, 56–67.

Pullen, A., Thanem, T., Tyler, M. and Wallenberg, L. (2016). Sexual politics, organizational practices: Interrogating queer theory, work and organization. *Gender, Work & Organization*, 23(1), pp. 1–6.

Salisbury, R. (2005). Books of the year II. *The Spectator*, 26 November.

Sarnecki, J. H. and O'Sickey, I. M. (eds.) (2004). *Subversive subjects: Reading Marguerite Yourcenar*. Madison: Farleigh Dickinson University Press.

Savigneau, J. (1993). Marguerite Yourcenar: Inventing a life. Chicago: Chicago University Press.

Sedgwick, E. K. (1990). *Epistemology of the closet*. New York, NY: Harvester Wheatsheaf.

Southwood, J. (2013). Marguerite Yourcenar: 'Feminine writer?' In: R. Lloyd, and J. Fornasiero, eds., *Magnificent obsessions: Honouring the lives of Hazel Rowley*. Newcastle upon Tyne: Cambridge Scholars Publishing, pp. 179–201.

Steyaert, C. (2010). Queering space. Heterotopic life in Derek Jarman's garden. *Gender, Work and Organization*, 17(1), 45–68.

Steyaert, C. (2015). Three women. A kiss. A life. On the queer writing of time in organization. *Gender, Work and Organization*, 22(2), 163–178.

Taat, M. (1986). La mer mêlée au soleil. *Il Confronto Letterario*, supplement to number, 5, pp. 59–67.

Taat, M. (2004). Is there no body on the scene of writing? Contemporary conceptions of textual practice in/and Yourcenar's paratexts. In: J. H. Sarnecki, and I. M.

O'Sickey, eds., *Subversive subjects: Reading Marguerite Yourcenar*. Madison: Farleigh Dickinson University Press, pp. 101–121.

Wittig, Monique. (1975). *The Lesbian Body*. New York: Morrow.

Yourcenar, M. (1981a). *The abyss*. New York, NY: Farrar, Straus, and Giroux.

Yourcenar, M. (1981b). *Coupe de grâce*. New York, NY: Farrar, Straus, and Giroux.

Yourcenar, M. (1981c). *Fires*. New York, NY: Farrar, Straus, and Giroux.

Yourcenar, M. (1984a). *Alexis: A novel*. New York, NY: Farrar, Straus and Giroux.

Yourcenar, M. (1984b). *With open eyes. Conversations with Matthieu Galey*. Boston: Beacon Press.

Yourcenar, M. (1991). *Anna, soror*. Paris: Gallimard.

Yourcenar, M. (2000). *Memoirs of Hadrian*. London: Penguin Books.

6 Witnessing Eve

Eve Kosofsky Sedgwick

Saara L. Taalas

Eve Kosofsky Sedgwick (1950–2009) is generally recognized as one of the most prominent writers in the development of queer theory. Sedgwick was a literary critic, poet, textile arts experimenter and social theorist. Her influence on literary criticism and social theory simply cannot be conveyed in its entirety, and let me be clear that this is not my intention. Rather I am inspired by Sedgwick who vividly states:

> I think many adults (and I am one of them) are trying, in our work, to keep faith with vividly remembered promises made to ourselves in childhood: promises to make invisible possibilities and desire visible; to make the tacit things explicit; to smuggle queer presentations in where it must be smuggled and, with the relative freedom of adulthood, to challenge queer-eradicating impulses frontally where they are to be so challenged.
>
> (Sedgwick, 1994, p. 3)

Rather, I would like to turn to the lingering question of why researchers in organization theory have not engaged with her work more broadly, although this is starting to change. Organization theory in recent years has shown a burgeoning interest in queer subjectivities and performativities (Parker, 2001; 2002; Rumens, 2016; 2017; 2018; Rippin, 2017), academic activism (Parker, 2001; Contu, 2017; Rippin, 2017) and the corporealities of affect (Fotaki, Kenny, and Vachhani, 2017).

In view of this recent interest in queer performativities and in affect and organization, Sedgwick's conceptual innovations certainly merit a closer look. However, I will not be conducting a full review of Sedgwick's works but rather focusing on Rumens's (2017) proposal that critical organization enquiry strikes up a friendship with queer theory. In this spirit, I would like to pick up some themes addressed in recent discussions on organization and see how Sedgwick's contribution might help 'destabilize management' (Parker, 2001). The purpose of this destabilization is to mobilize subject positions in regenerative ways. To this end, I will draw my main inspiration from Sedgwick's later works on queer performativity, which return to Austin's (1975/1997) speech-act theory, develop the concept of the periperformative and offer an alternative strategy for critical enquiry in reparative readings, a topic covered in her last book, *Touching Feeling – Affect, Pedagogy, Performative* (2003).

Anyone familiar with Sedgwick's work knows that the corporealities of writing and lived experience not only occupy a central role in her writing but also constitute the pivotal motivational thrust of her quest to pursue queer performativities. Perhaps surprisingly then, this chapter will carry no bold performatives referencing my own history in the AIDS activism of the early 1990s, or the normalizing treatments of breast cancer that Sedgwick herself calls 'adventures in the applied deconstruction' (1999) and that I similarly fought in first-person singular. I have chosen to *bear witness* to Sedgwick's remarkable creative scholarship and corporealities of a life lived in which ideas, body and histories collide but more importantly erotically entangle. This witness I bear is a periperformative kind that responds to the persistent normalizing that her queering strategies, tactical activism and conceptual entrepreneurship deconstructs. Performative in language calls for witness, whether willing or reluctant, in order to work. I am not a witness in the position of a third party. In this text, I am in the position of witness in the sense of someone who has lived through an event from its beginning to end (Agamben, 1999, p. 17).

In writing this chapter my body has not been a willing witness in the vicinities of Sedgwick. Sedgwick's queer performativity evokes not only the flourishing joy and sense of community in my life but also the grave death toll it holds. I have been unable to sleep, struggled with a complete inability to put thoughts to paper and been overwhelmed by grief. My body has simply witnessed too many deaths and losses for it not to revolt in this act of writing. However, my body's affective revolt is partly expected and ordinary. I turned queer activist in the face of a deadly epidemic and endured the normalizing agenda of a business school education, all of which are experiences that may not constitute what Sedgwick calls 'a miracle' but rather performances in the art of 'smuggling queer where it is not invited'. There is nothing more ordinary than queer survival, and 'everyone who survived has histories about how it was done' (Sedgwick, 1994, p. 1). Drawing on Deleuze, Probyn (2010) describes the corporealities of writing and the shame associated with survival, depicting the writing body as a battleground where ideas and experiences collide. While this notion may be overly heroic as regards literary struggles, engaging with Sedgwick's writing entails a struggle beyond the literary. Sedgwick relates shame and writing to the erotic dimension of the body and self. Her work profoundly problematizes identities, keeping them in constant motion/on the constant move. Although her project might not be philosophically or even politically programmic, in critical theory development one would be hard pressed to find another scholar in the vicinity of Deleuzean ontology so zestful in exploring modes of human flourishing in the face of adversity. Far from being theory development with a 'brain on a stick', Sedgwick's queer survival is situated in local and spatial corporealities and a joyful form of art (Rippin, 2017). She poses a great challenge to critical organiza-tion theory, asserting that surviving to expose adversity is not enough, one must also turn its materialities, textures, and experiences into resources for human flourishing. She proposes that the endless possibilities in situated corporealities and erotic joy have the potential to shift both subjectivities and politics.

Queer witness in language

> Jacques Derrida's and Judith Butler's important discussions of performativ-ity, for example, tend to proceed through analyses of its temporal complex-ity: iteration, citationality, the 'always ready', that whole valuable repertoire of conceptual shuttle movements that endlessly weave between the future and the past. By contrast, the localness of the periperformative is lodged in a metaphorics of space.
> [Two paragraphs in between.]
> It also strikes me that this spatialised 'around the performative' framework might offer some more tensile and nuanced ways than we've had so far of pushing further with the Althusserian concept of interpellation.
> [A paragraph in between.]
> But to do justice to the performative force of 'I dare you', as opposed to its arguably constative function of expressing 'attitudes', requires a disimpac-tion of the scene, as well as the act, of utterance. To begin with, although 'I dare you' ostensibly involves only a singular first and a singular sec-ond person, it effectually depends as well on the tacit demarcation of the space of a third-person plural, a 'they' of witness – whether or not literally present.
>
> (Sedgwick, 2003, pp. 68–69)

Organization theory has increasingly come to engage with the most promi-nent critical movements in twentieth-century social theory, including feministic critique, postcolonial study and, more recently, queer studies. Rumens (2017) points out that even critical management studies (CMS) has a poor track record in terms of an ability to address its own internal hierarchies and exclusions. Until recently, (Parker, 2001; 2002) no one in the organization theory field has engaged with Sedgwick's queer performativity as an attitude and a productive practice (Sedgwick, 1990). By the beginning of the new millennium humanistic and cultural studies had already explored queer theory at great length, with queer studies reaching a peak in the first part of the 1990s, a time when the study of queerness was closely intertwined with the political movements spurred by HIV/AIDS activism (Rumens, 2017; 2018). By the end of the 1990s, however, AIDS had already become a treatable illness in wealthy Western countries, and LGBT activists were already turning their sights elsewhere. The interest in queer studies and in Sedgwick's writing seems to be experiencing a modest renaissance in organization studies (see Rumens, 2017, pp. 235–237). This interest has been almost entirely driven by Sedgwick's *Epistemology of the Closet* (1990).

Parker (2001) aims the double barrel of Butler's *Gender Trouble* (1990) and Sedgwick's *Epistemology of the Closet* (1990) at the unshakable position management has held at the centre of the research field. Stressing his entirely academic aims of 'fucking management', he hopes to destabilize management as a category by using queer theory to jerk the field of critical management studies out of its reverie and compel it to become a politically engaged practice. Though Parker's aim is emancipatory, he is more at ease with Butler's work on identity politics than with Sedgwick's writing on the situational destabilizing of identity categories. This seems to be a common problem for organizational scholars engaged with Sedgwick's queer performativity. In a special issue in *Gender, Work, and Organization* (Pullen et. al. 2016a), Sedgwick is referenced in contributions concerning queer theory, the subjects of which range from occupational segregation (McDonald, 2016), aging LGBT employees (King, 2016), transgender politics (Muhr et. al., 2016), queering the queer in university education (Parker, 2016) and witnessing queer in business school (Rumens, 2016). In this body of work Sedgwick is positioned as an early example of thinking that questions the 'heteronormative matrix' of representation in the organization space rather than engaging with it. Perhaps the most Sedgwickian of this thinking is seen in an article reviewing recent developments in queer theory focused on sex and sex acts (Harding, 2016), a salient feature of Sedgwick's writing. Similarly, Parker (2001; 2016) engages with Sedgwick beyond identity politics, thus adopting bravado and theatricality as a style and mode of engagement as well as evoking joy and playfulness in the act of writing. Both Parker and Harding commit to a particularly Sedgwickian move of smuggling, where queerness is used to disrupt traditional interests and forms of writing in management and organization.

Instead of adopting Parker's (2001) direct and confrontational performative of calling readers to bear witness to his 'fucking management' as a bold act of deconstruction, Rumens (2017) suggests that critical management studies establish a more voluntary and open relation with queer studies, a kind of friendship. Rumens's suggestion resonates to a degree with Sedgwick's writing, for she observes that queer relations of friendship are not sanctioned by law or institutions and therefore considered private, rather than political (Sedgwick, 1994). In *Tendencies*, Sedgwick discusses friendship and in the last two chapters which are devoted to friends lost to AIDS, developing this notion of friendship as being continuous making, the witnessing of another over time in ways that are not complete but particular, what she calls a 'discontinuous projective space of desire euphemistically called friendship, love at a distance' (1994, p. 105). When Rumens raises the possibility of friendship, whether he hopes to evoke the erotic promise or the caution of distance is somewhat unclear. Could queering management go beyond identity and identification categories?

Sedgwick uses writing style as performance as a particular strategy of queering. For example, she continually utters 'I', the first-person singular, in her academic texts, poems, pedagogy and artwork. This aspect of productive queering as a form of activism cannot be told apart from her conceptual entrepreneurship on understanding performative utterance in language. Sedgwick sets out not only to trace performative utterances in language but also to impose their performative thrust in unexpected contexts and unorthodox relationships. Sedgwick famously uses the explicit performative 'I do', Austin's most prominent performative example, in contexts other than state-sanctioned marriage vows when she refers to any or many 'others' as a way of using a visceral thrust to make an affective connection and thus of evoking the strongest possible 'we'. These performative utterances have a certain theatricality that Sedgwick considered not as a falsity but as a necessary part of keeping queering at the centre of her work (2003, p. 8).

To gain spatial effect, explicit performatives must be sanctioned by the surrounding powers of the state and institutions and be witnessed. That Sedgwick keeps radical and disturbing possibilities continuously open, refusing to stay within the norm of academic writing as a particular genre, seems to be connected to her use of Austin's performative speech-act theory as a springboard. Instead of taking Austin's writing at face value, she seeks to disrupt and deconstruct it in ways similar to how she works with other literature. Sedgwick tends to treat philosophy as playfully as she treats literature. This oscillation between theory and its unmaking is central to Sedgwick's queering as a 'step sideways' from feminism and deconstruction

(2003, p. 8). Sedgwick invents concepts for understanding specific spatial organization in ways as yet unexplored in organization theory.

In developing her concept of perifperformatives, Sedgwick builds on Austin's (1975/1997) early works of illucatory utterances as parasidic (Sedgwick, 2003, p. 68). Sedgwick focuses on highly specific utterances in language – 'I promise . . .', 'I bequeath . . .', 'I christen . . .', 'I apologize . . .', 'I dare you . . .', 'I sentence you . . .' – as explicit performative utterances with local and spatial effects (2003, p. 4). Her project with periperformativity is to show the specifics of such utterances as producing localities of effects as well as to address the performative force of language utterance and its effects on specific corporeal materialities. Although her projects on the performative are often akin to the projects of deconstruction and feminist theory, Sedgwick's interest in developing the periperformative focuses not on the general nature of language utterances as productive with references in past and future but on its specificity and locality. Sedgwick's periperformatives are clusters and neighbourhoods of explicit performatives, everyday language utterances that are dependent on the explicit utterances.

Sedgwick thus posits a particular view of organization as a consequence of performative acts that call the witness of the norm community (willing or not) to the scenes of performative utterance that she terms neighbourhoods. Sedgwick uses nineteenth-century literature as diverse as Abraham Lincoln's 'Gettysburg Address', Henry James's *The Golden Bowl* and George Eliot's *Daniel Redonda* to provide examples of utterances that specifically diverge from Austin's formula for explicit utterances – the first-person singular present indicative active – but she also looks at all the utterances that gather around such utterances, many of the ordinary utterances of language. While we would perhaps like to see management as being a grand drama of explicit performative acts, in ordinary settings only periperformative spaces rely and lean on these language utterances. This makes management difficult to resist, overturn or queer. Business as usual is constructed in periperformative spatialities where 'they' are called to witness the enfolding of events in the explicit performatives of business and industry.

In her discussion of the periperformative in literature, Sedgwick draws a parallel between the slave trade in the United States and the institution of marriage in the UK. She sharply focuses on the selling of individuals as property and as a performative speech act that creates a powerful periperformative neighbourhood of relations in the vicinity of performatives fuelled by an ownership ideology. It is in these clusters, effects and neighbourhoods of performative utterances that power resides. Periperformative spatialities amplify and bridge performatives to the far corners of their neighbourhoods. Explicit performative utterance is unambiguous. For example, 'I promise' cannot simultaneously imply that a promise will be broken or a betrayal plotted (2003, p. 68). While the cause and effect between the utterance and a particular feeling in the act of uttering is explicitly dislinked, periperformativity can bridge effects of several performatives and create spatialities in and around their vicinity. This clustering of explicit performatives in close spatial proximity can linger and echo in a specific periperformative space, engendering an appearance of a kind of self-reference where identity categories collapse. However, unlike the project of deconstruction that aims to expose the explicit performatives of oppression, Sedgwick seems to indicate that while explicit performatives are at the core of institutions of ownership, and therefore also of management as ownership's function, it is the privileging by the state and institutions like the Church in the case of marriage that gives 'I do' its power, and the utterance must have a witnessing 'they' to achieve its effect. In the everyday organization periperformative space might be understood in terms of combined and relational effects that are situated in the evoked witness of 'they', be it real or only existing in language use, and in the acute corporealities of experiencing the effect of such a performative in the loneliness of 'you'.

It is the situated and necessary witnessing of 'they' that gives explicit performatives their visceral thrust and corporeality over 'you'. As Sedgwick explains when a woman is exhibited as a Greek slave: 'but the dramaturgically spatialized and affect-defining *scene* of forced display and the act of *sale*' (2003, p. 80).

Pullen et. al. (2017) give an example of exactly this kind of periperformative organizational space in their discussion of affective politics in gendered organization when recounting a story in which one of the authors is pressured to perform for university benefactors in a situation where they were unable to prepare or decline and instead was suddenly singled out to perform their academic scholarship on a moment's notice.

Ahmed (2010) raises a similar question about the consequences of explicit performatives in relationship to normative assumptions of happiness. She is particularly interested in the speech act 'I just want you to be happy', and in happiness as a performative object, something permanently beyond the reach of queer or gay. Similarly, unhappiness as melancholy is attached to immigrants as a kind of 'reluctance to let go' of past unhappiness. Ahmed's treatment echoes Sedgwick's example of the marriage vow 'I do' as a state and institutionally sanctioned performative that queer people are called on to witness, something that might be difficult or painful, but most importantly, politically difficult to resist by simply refusing such witness. Ahmed goes even further, providing an example whereby refusing such witness as part of 'they' would break not only social norms but also other people's possibility of being happy in marriage. The witness is evoked by the performative without the consent of the witness, as the institution, social norms and 'the happy couple' are implied in the performative's utterance as given. Ahmed suggests that such 'happy objects' are delusive and that preserving positive affects might be counter to subjective freedoms. She goes on to suggest that letting go of 'happy objects' might be a necessary step in putting behind the exclusion causing the unhappiness. I stop Ahmed there and step aside before she goes on to criticize affirmative feminism for looking for happier affects. I pause briefly because she has just presented a reparative reading of one situation of racism without the result having to be built on universal happiness and the experience of feel-good as an outcome. Sedgwick's tactics of reparative readings differ from the pursuit of happiness in affirmative feminism or positive psychology, for she would propose a 'step aside' before the story gets the normalized ending. By side-stepping Sedgwick proposes a reparative reading even if it is not a complete object, incorporating even experiences of normative oppression to form new constellations that might not be happy ends but that are joyous tactics of resistance to combat normalizing tendencies. I will return to this point after a note on affect.

Witnessing body

> I do mean to nominate the [Henry] James of New Your edition prefaces as a kind of prototype of, not 'homosexuality', but 'queerness', or queer performativity. In this usage, 'queer performativity' is the name of a strategy for the production of meaning and being, in relation to the affect shame and to the later and related fact of stigma.
>
> (Sedgwick, 2003, p. 61)

Sedgwick's work has been associated with the affective turn taken in literary criticism and cultural and arts studies in the mid-1990s, and the influence of affect has recently been recognized in organization studies as well (Fotaki, Kenny, and Vachhani, 2017, special issue editorial). Despite this recent interest in affect, Sedgwick's work continues to have a greater influence on thinking in human geographies, economic geography and the performing arts than on organization theory. At first glance, this might appear to be the result of some misguided interpretations of essentialism, akin to the limited attention that embodiment is given in organization studies.

> These theorists are gripped by the notion that most philosophers and critics in the past (Kantians, neo-Kantians, Habermasians) have overvalued the role of reason and rationality in politics, ethics, and aesthetics, with the result that they have given too flat, i.e. 'unlayered', or

disembodied an account of the ways in which people actually form
their political opinions and judgments.

(Leys, 2011, p. 436)

Disembodiment in mainstream organization theory is gaining increasing
critical attention (Hassard et. al. 2000; Hancock and Tyler, 2001; Thanem
and Knights, 2010). The dangers of leaving body aside have been studied
in organization analysis (Hassard, Holliday, and Willmott, 2000), and more
recent scholarly works have addressed the tendency to approach the corporealities of the body from a position of ignorance, or to organize, manage,
manipulate and control the body (Knights and Thanem, 2010). It is against
this broader backdrop of the corporeal in critical management studies that
Sedgwick's work on affect becomes relevant in the latest discussions surrounding the relationship of affect and emotion in organization (Fotaki,
Kenny, and Vachhani, 2017).

Sedgwick's work is inspired by psychologist Tomkins's (Sedgwick and
Frank, 1995) affect theory. Tomkins was preoccupied with understanding
embodiment and affect not only in terms of Freudian drives but as a separate system innate to all individuals. Tomkins view of affects as changing in intensity and emerging into cognitive consciousness through their
visceral thrust – feelings as rewarding, punishing and neutral – had an
enduring influence on Sedgwick's work (Sedgwick and Frank, 1995;
Sedgwick, 2003). Tomkins's system pairs affects interest–excitement,
enjoyment–joy, surprise–startlement, distress–anguish, contempt–disgust,
anger–rage and shame–humiliation. Sedgwick's work focused on how
intense and urgent affects penetrate cognitive consciousness – their performative thrust – and whether affects can take habitual identifications
that are under pressure and shift them in new directions, thus creating new
ways of looking at identity politics (2003, p. 64). Her primary empirical
work was to connect shame and pride and to explore productive shame
as pleasure interrupted. Sedgwick and Frank (1995) position affect as
suspended between the individual and social. Sedgwick sees affect as a
'free radical' that can shift subjectivities outside normative boundaries,
even permanently. In her discussion on habitual shame (2003, p. 62), she
explores the subjectivities that form when norm boundaries are broken.
Pivotal to Sedgwick is the relationship of shame and pride to queer performativity, and how intensifying affect like habitual shame might destabilize identities. The view of shame as productive is key here. Sedgwick
is interested in the connection of shame to politics insofar as it 'generates
and legitimates a place of identity' without giving 'identity space a stand-
ing of an essence' (2003, p. 64). Shame is contagious and productive,
which makes it political and in Sedgwick's reading fuels activism.

Probyn (2004) takes inspiration from Sedgwick and Frank's (1995) treatment of shame as pleasure interrupted, showing a particular interest in the contagiousness of affect in the formation of community. 'They [affects] are also both intensely individual and social; more importantly, and as I argue, they undo any opposition that relies on alignments of private/public' (Probyn, 2004, p. 239). Probyn takes a Deleuzean perspective in exploring shame as productive when she analyzes affect in relation to First Nation's sacred Uluru and Australia's iconic Ayers Rock. Her work on productive shame and pride is programmic (Probyn, 2004; 2010).

Affect theory critics (Hemmings, 2005; Leys, 2011) spot a specific problem with Sedgwick's notion that the affect system is 'autotelic' to cognition and therefore separate from emotion. This way of understanding the workings of body-mind and the underlying assumption that systemic and largely automatic biological responses are responsible for the degree of neural firing sets the cognitive mind as something that simply witnesses the body's affects. This view has been critiqued in the social sciences and, more recently, even in the neurosciences (Leys, 2011). However, this assumption of the anti-intentionality of affect is largely shared with Massumi's and Deleuze's inspired analysis of affect.

> Although at first sight the work of Tomkins – or Ekman, or Damasio – might appear to be too reductive for the purposes of those cultural theorists indebted to Deleuzean ideas about affect, there is in fact a deep coherence between the views of both groups.
>
> (Leys, 2011, 443)

Tomkins's affect theory is inspired by a psychologist from the 1890s, novelist Henry James's brother, William James, who was inspired by Spinoza. Recently, parallel influences running from Spinoza via James to Deleuze (1997) and Massumi (1995, 2002) have been shown to be far more complex than previously thought, for which reason it might be time to re-evaluate Sedgwick's role in bridging the biological sciences and humanities study (Lays, 2011).

Sedgwick herself seemed quite unconcerned about the question of affect and its roots, preferring to invest her energies in queer embodiment and the connection of sensuality to evolving subjectivities and, particularly, to destabilizing identities. What appears to be emerging from the more contemporary work in both the social sciences and neurosciences is that affect intensities are contextually interpreted in social meaning-making and labelling that vary in performative contexts, historical situations and cultural settings (Leys, 2011; Nørholm Just et. al. 2017). Sedgwick makes no contribution to labelling categories, avoiding them at all costs, but rather relentlessly pursues a research programme that would insist on not only opening up to biology in the humanities and social sciences but also exploring the relationship of experiences of the sensual self, of communities and of emerging politics beyond mere mechanics. In Sedgwick's perspective, failure to connect these aspects in analysis would run the risk of reproducing anew the body-mind divide that has persisted in social theory (2003, p. 114). It is in this epistemological critique that she calls for a research agenda of reparative readings as a form of critique and activism (Sedgwick, 2003, pp. 123–151).

Reparative witness

> The elaboration of Melanie Klein's notion of the reparative was one of Sedgwick's great later contributions. Sedgwick famously outlined the reparative as a way out of the rote dominance of paranoid readings that traded in the hermeneutics of suspicion. Reperative was meant to help us consider something other than the unveiling of that thing we kind of already knew anyway. The reparative is a theoretical stance where we use our own physic and imaginative resources to reconstruct partial or dangerously incomplete objects that structure our reality into workable sense of wholeness. The reconstructed sense of an object offers us a kind of sustenance and comfort.
>
> (Muñoz, 2013, p. 110)

Sedgwick's *Paranoid Reading and Reparative Reading or You're So Paranoid, You Probably Think This Essay Is About You* (2003, pp. 123–152) offers her alternative to critical inquiry. Although the idea of reparative reading was originally raised in reference to queer studies and the consequences of deconstruction to precarious subjectivities, feminist scholars (e.g. Love, 2010; Hanson, 2011; Wiegman, 2014) have lately picked up the idea. It has been suggested that this is due to recent moves to understand how affect binds and how a scholarship community 'makes claims on the political landscape of the present by taking the present as an affectively resonant scene for ongoing debate about politics, agency, temporality, and the value and utility of criticism itself' (Wiegman, 2014, 6).

Sedgwick opens her call for reparative readings by recollecting her conversation with an AIDS activist and scholar, Cindy Patton. Would it have mattered if we had known for certain that the AIDS crisis was caused by an HIV virus that had escaped from some laboratory? Patton replies: 'What would we know then that we don't already know?' (2003, p. 123). This example brings us directly to Sedgwick's central argument that unveiling systematic and ongoing oppression does not spawn any necessary epistemological or narrative consequences.

Currently, some distinct moves are being made in organization theory to turn away from the 'hermeneutics of suspicion' as being imperative to the search for embodied alternatives to scholarly criticism and instead turn towards a 'hermeneutics of recovery of meaning' (p. 125). For example, recent projects coming from the contemporary perspectives of feminist and queer studies include an inquiry into affective leadership that builds on affective corporealities and ethics (Knights, 2017, 2018; Munro and Thanem, 2018; Thanem and Wallenber, 2015) and a challenge to existing practices within critical management studies (Pullen, Rhodes, and Thanem, 2017), both of which revisit and reject the 'habitual practice' of critical theory of stopping at the stage of revelation. These projects are seeking to replace the suspicion at the methodological centre of critical scholarly practice and create a more communal and ethical centre connected to embodied scholarly activism.

With respect to scholarly activism, the role of Sedgwick's pedagogical work has been largely overlooked. Rippin (2017) picks up this important aspect of Sedgwick's late contribution in which Sedgwick did some pedagogical work on picture-book workshops, positioning love and the textures of materials like textiles as reparative practices at the core of critical scholarship. Rippin goes to extreme lengths to trace in minute detail the practices of Sedgwick's workshops, even doing embodied experimentation to recreate some of the methods lost. It is an impressive study into the recovery of meaning and the assembly of resources and practices for survival. Reparative readings akin to Rippin's evoke the only ethical position Sedgwick would acknowledge was available to a researcher: a focus on protecting and celebrating marginalized, precarious and queer subject positions by witnessing their flourishing, power and creativity.

Sedgwick's analysis of paranoid reading continues to be insightful in two ways. First, it offers a critique of the dominant deconstructive and critical research practices motivated and driven by exposure for the sake of static 'truths' that offer no insights beyond the expected. Perhaps identity politics based from the outset on doomed positions of oppression leave little room for emancipation and change, or even survival, for the vulnerable. Sedgwick invokes her fellow activist's words as a reminder that – just as the panic-fuelled suspicion of Big Pharma conspiracy engendered AIDS survival – an obsession with 'truth' continues neither to be able to stem the spread of HIV nor to turn general public opinion regarding the victims of disease or tell us much about its stigma. Second, reparative readings and activism offer not only comfort but also map tactics for survival and alternative resources for it. Alas, 'truth' of these tactical subjectivities and practices are perhaps precarious but nevertheless no less true and worth witnessing (e.g. Hallas, 2009). While such tactical subjectivities rarely offer strategic solutions, are rarely in synch with permanent identity categories and are seldom institutionally sanctioned, they may offer resources to keep up the fight to make the invisible visible and drive a change in politics. Reparative readings are crucial resources for vulnerable and temporal subjectivities in and around organizations and academia.

Conclusions

Recent years have seen a rise in academic activism in the business school context (Contu, 2017). While academic activism in itself is hardly foreign to social studies and prominent in the writing of thinkers like Foucault (Munro, 2014), activism has been largely missing from business school scholarship until now as sustainability networks become established, a women's network and a decolonializing alliance in critical management studies emerge, and diversity awareness days are organized (Contu, 2017). While critical scholarship on organization was a writing-only community in the 1990s, it is increasingly becoming writing and public scholarship that populates business school spaces once more for activism. Sedgwick's work was involved in AIDS activism, and her writing on queer performativity and affective communities could not be separated from that experience. Even her poetry, artwork and corporealities of living played a central role in her broad conceptual work. Sedgwick was not only a Proust scholar but also an inspirational activist in her writing, art and pedagogy.

As the events of the #MeToo social media campaign unfold, Sedgwick's writing raises the question of whether queering can be considered a style or an approach outside the LGBTQ community or should be sensitive to its roots (Pullen et. al., 2016b). During the outbreak of the AIDS epidemic in the 1980s and the growing AIDS activism of the early 1990s, Sedgwick emerged as an academic activist and a voice of boldness in the face of adversity, breaking the taboo of silence around homosexuality and sociality, sex and the possibilities of the erotic self. She became central to a field of research we now commonly refer to as queer studies, putting a particular stress on corporeality and the multitude of critical theoretical developments and keeping identities and politics permanently on the move. Today, her writing continues to be one of the most influential voices in cultural studies on queer performativity and affect. It seems that her work continues to influence feminism and social studies scholarship that transcends/outside strict gender politics (e.g. Probyn, 2004; 2010). This chapter has aimed to witness Sedgwick's influence in our understanding of corporealities in queer performativity, affect and the epistemologies of critical thought, connecting them to the recent debates regarding critical organizational inquiry.

Sedgwick's scholarship did not stop at queer performativity, and it is at this precise juncture that she becomes Eve, not only a scholar who was starting to get famous for her work but as someone who took risks and was not afraid of controversy (Wiegman, 2012). Perhaps this made her go further than most literary scholars. After witnessing queer performativity and resisting notions of identity categorizations, Eve adamantly, untiringly, went on to devise resources for survival in her conceptual work, activism, poems and artwork. She has shown how criticism can be a work of love and restoration. I saw the power of this in the midst of the fight to halt the genocide that was AIDS nearly 30 years ago. Eve's writing became a beacon of light in the darkness for many. I see a similar build-up of resources in her 18-year battle with breast cancer, a battle that she finally lost. Although unvictorious, her deconstruction of the insufferable normalizing practices of cancer treatments has inspired me and others to fight the double impact of both the disease and its normalizing treatments. She became the ultimate witness. But unlike most firsthand witnesses, her voice continues to be heard. This is my witness of Eve.

Recommended reading

Original text by Sedgwick

Archive: Eve Kosofsky Sedgwick artworks. Available at: http://evekosofskysedgwick. net/art/artworks/

Key academic text

Gond, J-P., Cabantous, L., Harding, N. and Learmonth, M. (2016). What do we mean by performativity in organizational and management theory? The uses and abuses of performativity. *International Journal of Management Reviews*, 18, pp. 440–463. https://doi.org/10.1111/ijmr.12074. Available at: https://onlinelibrary.wiley.com/doi/full/10.1111/ijmr.12074

Accessible resource

Video: Honoring Eve Symposium, Boston University College of Arts & Sciences. (October 31, 2009). 'Affect and Reparative Reading' Panel with J. Keith Vincent (moderator), Jonathan Flatley, Heather Love, and Tavia Nyong'o on Sedgwick's Paranoid reading and reparative reading. In: *Touching feeling: Affect, performativity, pedagogy*. Durham: Duke University Press, 2003, pp. 123–151. Available at: www.bu.edu/honoringeve/about-the-symposium/affect-and-reparative-reading/

References

Ahmed, S. (2010). Happy objects. In: M. Gregg, and G. J. Seigworth, eds., *The affect theory reader*. Durham and London: Duke University Press, pp. 29–51.
Agamben, G. (1999). *Remnants of auschwitz: The witness and the archive*. New York, NY: Zone Books.

Austin, J. L. (1975/1997). *How to do things with words*. Cambridge: Harvard University Press.

Contu, A. (2017). The point is to change it – Yes, but in what direction and how? *Organization*, 25(2), pp. 282–293.

Deleuze, G. (1997). *Essays critical and clinical*. Minneapolis, MN: University of Minnesota Press.

Fotaki, M., Kenny, K. and Vachhani, S. J. (2017). Thinking critically about affect in organization studies: Why it matters. *Organization*, 24(1), pp. 3–17.

Hallas, R. (2009). *Reframing bodies: AIDS, bearing witness, and the queer moving image*. Durham, NC: Duke University Press.

Harding, N. (2016). New directions in queer theory: Recent theorizing in the work of Lynne Huffer, Leo Bersani & Adam Phillips, and Lauren Berlant & Lee Edelman. *Gender Work and Organization*, 23(1), pp. 74–83.

Hanson, E. (2011). The future's eve: Reparative reading after Sedgwick. *South Atlantic Quarterly*, 110(1), pp. 101–119.

Hancock, P. and Tyler, M. (2001). *Work, postmodernism and organization: A critical introduction*. London: Sage.

Hassard, J., Holliday, R. and Willmott, H. (2000). *Body and organization*. London: Sage.

Hemmings, C. (2005). Invoking affect. Cultural theory and the ontological turn. *Cultural Studies*, 19(5), 548–567.

King, S. (2016). Queer categories: Queer(y)ing the identification 'Older Lesbian, Gay and/or Bisexual (LGB) Adults' and its implications for organizational research, policy and practice. *Gender Work and Organization*, 23(1), pp. 7–18.

Knights, D. (2017). Leadership, masculinity and ethics in financial services. In: J. Storey, J. Hartley, J- L., Denis, P. T. Hart, and D. Ulrich, eds., *The Routledge companion to leadership*. London: Routledge.

Knights, D. (2018). What's more effective than affective leadership? Searching for embodiment in leadership research and practice. In: C. Mabey, and D. Knights, eds., *'Leadership Matters?': Finding voice, connection and meaning in the 21st century*. London and New York, NY: Routledge.

Leys, R. (2011). The turn to affect: A critique. *Critical Inquiry*, 37(3) (Spring 2011), pp. 434–472.

Love, H. (2010). Truth and consequences: On paranoid reading and reparative reading. *Criticism*, 52(2), pp. 235–241.

Massumi, B. (1995). The autonomy of affect. *Cultural Critique* (31). *The Politics of Systems and Environments*, Part II, pp. 83–109.

Massumi, B. (2002). *Parables for the virtual: Movement, affect, sensation*. Durham: Duke University Press.

McDonald, J. (2016). Occupational segregation research: Queering the conversation. *Gender, Work, and Organization*, 9(2), pp. 19–35.

Muhr, S., Sullivan, K. R. and Rich, G. (2016). Situated transgressiveness: Exploring one transwoman's lived experiences across three situated contexts. *Gender, Work, and Organization*, 9(2), pp. 52–70.

Muñoz, J. E. (2013). Race, sex, and the incommensurate: Gary Fisher with Eve Kosofsky Sedgwick. In: E. H. Yekani, E. Kilian, and B. Michaelis, eds., *Queer futures: Reconsidering ethics, activism, and the political*. Farnham: Ashgate, pp. 103–115.

Munro, I. (2014). Organizational Ethics and Foucault's 'Art of Living': Lessons from Social Movement Organizations. *Organization Studies*, 35(8), 1127–1148.

Munro, I. and Thanem, T. (2018). The ethics of affective leadership: Organizing good encounters without leaders. *Business Ethics Quarterly*, 28(1), pp. 51–69.

Nørholm, J. S., Muhr, S. L. and Burø, T. (2017). Queer matters – Reflections on the critical potential of affective organizing. In: A. Pullen, N. Harding, and M. Phillips, eds., *Feminists and queer theorists debate the future of critical management studies (Dialogues in Critical Management Studies, Volume 3)*. Bingley: Emerald Publishing Limited, pp. 203–226.

Parker, M. (2001). Fucking management: Queer, theory, and reflexivity. *Ephemera*, 1(1), pp. 36–53.

Parker, M. (2002). Queering management and organization. *Gender, Work, and Organization*, 9(2), pp. 146–166.

Parker, M. (2016). Queering queer. *Gender, Work & Organization*, 23(1), pp. 71–73.

Probyn, E. (2004). Everyday shame. *Cultural Studies*, 18(2–3), pp. 328–249.

Probyn, E. (2010). Writing shame. In: M. Gregg, and G. J. Seigworth, eds., *The affect theory reader*. Durham and London: Duke University Press, pp. 29–51.

Pullen, A., Rhodes, C. and Thanem, T. (2017). Affective politics in gendered organizations: Affirmative notes on becoming-woman. *Organization*, 24(1), pp. 105–123.

Pullen, A., Thanem, T., Tyler, M. and Wallenberg, L. (2016a). Sexual politics, organizational practices: Interrogating queer theory, work and organization. *Gender Work and Organization*, 23(1), pp. 1–6.

Pullen, A., Thanem, T., Tyler, M. and Wallenberg, L. (2016b). Queer endings/queer beginnings. *Gender Work and Organization*, 23(1), pp. 84–87.

Rippin, A. (2017). Writing with eve: Queering paper. In: A. Pullen, N. Harding, and M. Phillips, eds., *Feminists and queer theorists debate the future of critical management studies* (Dialogues in Critical Management Studies, Vol. 3). Bingley: Emerald Publishing Limited, pp. 171–194.

Rumens, N. (2016). Towards queering the business school: A research agenda for advancing lesbian, gay, bisexual and trans perspectives and issues. *Gender, Work and Organization*, 23(1), pp. 36–51.

Rumens, N. (2017). Critical management studies, queer theory and the prospect of a queer friendship. In: A. Pullen, N. Harding, and M. Phillips, eds., *Feminists and queer theorists debate the future of critical management studies (Dialogues in Critical Management Studies, Volume 3)*. Bingley: Emerald Publishing Limited, pp. 227–247.

Rumens, N. (2018). *Queer business. Queering organization sexualities*. (Advances in Critical Diversities). New York, NY and Abingdon: Routledge.

Sedgwick, E. K. (1990). *Epistemology of the closet*. Berkeley: University of California Press.

Sedgwick, E. K. (1994). *Tendencies*. London: Routledge.

Sedgwick, E. K. (1999). *A dialogue on love*. Boston, MA: Beacon Press.

Sedgwick, E. K. (2003). *Touching feeling: Affect, pedagogy, performativity*. Durham: Duke University Press.

Sedgwick, E. K. and Frank, A. (eds.) (1995). *Shame and its sisters: A Silvan Tomkins reader*. Durham: Duke University Press.

Thanem, T. and Knights, D. (2012). 'Feeling and speaking through our gendered bodies: Embodied self-reflection and research practice in organisation studies', *International Journal of Work Organisation and Emotion*, 5(1): 91–108.

Thanem, T. and Wallenberg, L. (2015). 'What can bodies do? Reading Spinoza for an affective ethics of organizational life'. *Organization*, 22(2), pp. 235–250.

Wiegman, R. (2012). Eve, at a distance. *Trans-Scripts*, 2(2012), pp. 157–175.

Wiegman, R. (2014). The times we're in: Queer feminist criticism and the reparative 'turn'. *Feminist Theory*, 15(1), pp. 4–25.

7 J. Jack Halberstam

Nick Rumens

J. Jack Halberstam is not a figure commonly associated with management and organization studies (MOS), yet there are significant signs that the concepts 'female masculinity' and 'queer failure' are being mobilized by MOS scholars interested in writing on gender, fluidity and embodiment. Closely allied with trans* studies and queer theory, and often bridging the two domains, J. Jack Halberstam's writing cultivates provocative forms of gender politics that have no truck with worn-out, hollow neoliberal notions of diversity, individualism and inclusivity. For example, Halberstam's work on trans* identities and bodies, female masculinity, queer failure and gaga feminism incites us to reimagine gender politics anew, compelling us to (re) engage with themes of emancipation based on 'insurgent, irrational revelry' (2012a, p. 148), plumbing the hidden depths of 'low. culture' (e.g. children's films) and reinventing notions that have traditionally negative connotations like 'failure' and 'forgetting' (2011).

The reader will become acquainted with Halberstam, who refuses to make concessions to neoliberal gender politics, in particular the essentialist modes of living and relating as gendered subjects that are conditioned and codified by them. At the same time, Halberstam asks bigger questions of us, about how we can transcend the neoliberal 'chimera of individualism' (2012a, p. 141) in ways that provide glimpses into something else that we can call the 'future'. Put differently, an animating impulse throughout Halberstam's work is the desire to explore how individuals may live life otherwise, beyond the constraints and regulations of hetero-norms. Accordingly, heteronormativity is a key concept and object of analysis in Halberstam's writing, commonly understood as 'the elemental form of human association, as the very model of inter-gender relations, as the indivisible basis of all community, and as the means of reproduction without which society wouldn't exist' (Warner, 1993, p. vii). Heteronormativity is a normative regime that variously reproduces the heterosexual/homosexual binary within culture, institutions, values and assumptions. For instance, heteronormativity is apparent in the Western cultural bias that privileges opposite-sex relationships, prevailing expectations about how men and women ought to dress and behave, and the importance of monogamy within marriage, to mention just a few examples. Halberstam's scholarship and politics contests the heterosexual/homosexual binary, problematizing how heterosexuality is normalized as 'natural', 'neutral' and 'healthy', while non-heterosexual and gender 'deviant' subjects are often but not always designated 'abnormal', 'unhealthy' and 'deviant'.

To begin unpacking Halberstam's contributions in that regard, this chapter starts by briefly sketching out Halberstam's background and the academic context in which key works such as *Female Masculinity* (1998), *In a Queer Time and Place: Transgender Bodies, Subcultural Lives* (2005a), *The Queer Art of Failure* (2011) and *Gaga Feminism* (2012a) have gained luminosity within the humanities and cultural studies and beyond.

Background and context

Halberstam graduated from the University of California, Berkeley in the mid-1980s with a BA in English before attaining an MA in English from the University of Minnesota, Minneapolis. Halberstam was later awarded a PhD in English literature from the University of Minnesota before embarking on an accomplished academic career. Currently Full Professor of American Studies and Ethnicity, Comparative Literature and Gender Studies at the University of Southern California, Halberstam's writing has to date exhibited a wide scope of research interests in the field of gender politics, queer theory, film and literature. For example, this corpus of work covers monsters and horror films (1991; 1993; 1995); drag kings (2001; 1997; Volcano and Halberstam, 1999); female masculinity (2012b; 1998); transgender bodies and trans* issues (2018; 2005a); queer notions of time and space (2005a; 2003a); shame and white gay masculinity (2005b); developments within queer theory (2008; 2003b); queering failure (2011); and the concept of 'gaga' and its relation with a politics of anti-normativity and anarchy (2012a; 2012b; 2013). This selection is by no means a complete bibliography; rather, it is intended to provide an overview of the principal topics that have occupied Halberstam. Additionally, Halberstam is a prolific writer on Bully Bloggers, an online queer word art group comprising academics interested in the term 'queer'.

Being someone who self-identifies as gender ambiguous (e.g. writing under the names of 'Judith Halberstam' and 'J. Jack Halberstam'), Halberstam is often labelled a prominent queer and trans* theorist who continues to play a leading role in advancing knowledge on trans* issues. Thus, the switch in names betrays a serious concern with the power effects of naming:

> I mostly go by 'Jack' nowadays, although people who have known me for a really long time and some family members still call me Judith. Then there are a few people, my sister included, who call me 'Jude'. I have debated switching out Jack for Jude to try to compress the name ambiguity into a more clear opposition between Judith and Jude. But then again – and contrary to my personality or my politics – when it comes to names and pronouns, I am a bit of a free floater. This goes against my instincts and my general demeanor – I don't hang in the middle ground on much, not politically, not socially, not in terms of culture, queer issues, feminism or masculinity. I am a person of strong opinions so why, oh why, do I insist on being loosey goosey about pronouns?
>
> (www.jackhalberstam.com/bio/)

Halberstam goes on to say that the to and fro between pronouns maintains an openness and elasticity that reflects Halberstam's contingent relation to gender. Having not transitioned in a formal sense, Halberstam asserts that 'floating gender pronouns capture well the refusal to resolve my gender ambiguity that has become a kind of identity for me' (www.jackhalberstam. com/bio/). This sense of gender fluidity is a recurring theme throughout Halberstam's scholarship in exploring, for example, the importance of naming in knowledge production on trans* identities and genders. Halberstam writes in *Trans: A Quick and Quirky Account of Gender Variability*, the presence of an asterisk after the term trans (e.g. trans*) staves off 'any sense of knowing in advance what the meaning of this or that gender variant form may be' (2018, p. 4). The desire to sustain fluidity in how genders are categorized, understood and ascribed meaning is motivated, in part, to ensure trans* people are the 'authors of their own categorizations' (2018, p. 4). Indeed, at a time when hetero gender norms continue to be castigated for constraining rather than enabling liveable gendered lives (Butler, 2004; Halberstam, 2018), and in a context of a bewildering array of gender variants, language often falls short in Halberstam's view for naming new forms of gender variance: 'Yet we have so few words for these new and often quite welcome complications that accompany massive social shifts' (2012a, p. xviii). Crucially, Halberstam's research has helped to pioneer the exploration of trans* identities, genders and bodies from a perspective of 'relationality', which articulates trans* not as a descriptor for 'an identity, but a relation between people, within a community, or within intimate bonds' (2005a, p. 49). Viewed relationally, Halberstam argues that the term trans* can channel attention toward a politics of recognition; more precisely, understanding how gendered subjects are placed within 'particular forms of recognition' (2005a, p. 49) that enable and foreclose opportunities to live meaningful lives beyond hetero-norms.

The academic context in which Halberstam's work has been written is key for understanding its influence, in particular within cultural studies and the humanities. Much of Halberstam's scholarship is positioned within the burgeoning canon of trans* studies and queer theory literature. Halberstam is often linked to queer theory, not least because of the antinormative impulse that underwrites Halberstam's research. Briefly, queer theory can be understood as a set of conceptual resources that have been forged in poststructuralism, radical feminism and gay and lesbian studies. It has also been shaped by gay, lesbian and queer political activism of the 1980s and 1990s that celebrated 'queer' (non-normative) sexualities and genders, and campaigned for social transformation in key social institutions and arenas (e.g. education, employment), to overcome the heteronormativity 'queer' people experience in everyday life. Within the academy, queer theory is often said to possess an anti-normative compulsion, evident, for example, in how it persistently questions prevailing, heteronormative ways of understanding gender, sex, the body, sexuality and sexual desire (Edelman, 2004; Warner, 1993). Vibrating in this chord, Halberstam's work is innovative, uncompromising and unsettling in how it both recuperates and envisions alternative non-normative genders, gender relations and new ways of comprehending what the future can become.

Key concepts and contributions

This section elucidates three critical concepts developed in Halberstam's writing that variously illustrate the theme of gender, fluidity and embodiment. These include female masculinities, failure as queer negativity and gaga feminism.

Female masculinities

Halberstam's popularization of the concept of female masculinity for queer and trans* studies scholars is premised on the argument that female masculinity 'is a specific gender with its own cultural history rather than a derivative of male masculinity' (1998, p. xx). *Female Masculinity* (1998) is a seminal work in that regard, problematizing the hidebound relationship between men and masculinity that has blinded us to a history of women performing masculinity for over 200 years. Exposing and problematizing the normative and protected status of male masculinity, Halberstam urges us to embrace a non-essentialist notion of gender fluidity, arguing that 'masculinity must not and cannot and should not reduce down to the male body and its effects' (1998, p. 1). This assertion invites us to read female masculinity outside the confines of the male body, and thus reveals the poststructuralist theoretical underpinning of female masculinity, conceptualized as an effect of discourse (see also Butler, 1990; 1993). Halberstam (1998) acknowledges Butler's work on the 'lesbian phallus' that locates the potentiality of masculine power within a female form but argues that it needs 'embodiment'. Here, then, Halberstam illustrates the diverse embodiments of female masculinities by, for example, exhuming representations of 'butch' women in literature and film, and examining the cultural phenomena of 'drag kings'. Such illustrations of female masculinity serve at least two important functions: (1) to counter the negative readings of female masculinity, such as when the masculine 'butch' woman provokes discomfort and, thus, must be rejected so male masculinity can appear to be the 'real' thing; and (2) to affirm female masculinity so 'masculine girls and women do not have to wear their masculinity as a stigma but can infuse it with a sense of pride and indeed power' (1998, p. xi).

Illustrating both, Halberstam provides a reading of female masculinity in the 1995 James Bond film *GoldenEye*. Halberstam concentrates on *GoldenEye* because it is the first Bond film in which M is played by a woman (Dame Judi Dench), and who, for Halberstam, performs a more convincing masculinity than Bond. Examining the hetero-masculinity of both James Bond (played at the time by Pierce Brosnan) and M, Halberstam reads Bond's masculinity as an instantiation of 'prosthetic masculinity' (1998, p. 3), embodied in the technical wizardry of the gadgets, cars and weapons which has become synonymous with James Bond. Artificial paraphernalia signify Bond's masculinity; stripped of these 'toys', Halberstam argues, 'Bond has very little propping up his performance of masculinity' (1998, p. 4). In contrast, M, read by Halberstam as a 'noticeably Butch older woman' (1998, p. 3), performs masculinity in a more convincing manner, scything straight to the heart of Bond's engineered masculinity by calling him a 'dinosaur' and berating him for his sexism, then lecturing him and the audience about how sexism is redundant in the traditionally masculine work of the modern spy. In so doing, M reveals Bond's masculinity for what it is – performatively constituted through gender norms that belong to a bygone era in espionage. Halberstam points out that Bond's discursive performance of masculinity is not just reliant on an unending supply of toys, but also 'minority' subordinate masculinities personified by the likes of M whose performance of female masculinity, ironically, outperforms Bond in the masculinity stakes. Crucially, Halberstam does not suggest that female masculinity is a more authentic masculinity; rather, Halberstam demonstrates how women can perform masculinities in their own right, resisting heteronormativity and its regulatory gender norms.

The theme of gender embodiment is interrogated again in *In a Queer Time and Place* (2005a), a text which examines gender variance and complexity in the cultural representations of trans* genders and bodies in film, art and society. Arguably, Halberstam's greatest contributions to advancing knowledge on gender, fluidity and embodiment are located at the site of trans* genders and bodies. Like *Female Masculinity, In a Queer Time and Place* is a restorative project that aims to bring trans* bodies and genders into focus, as sites of gender complexity that are mediated by time and space. Using film for illustrative and analytical purposes, Halberstam asks: can there be a transgender gaze? This question is apposite in the light of the visibility of transgender bodies in mainstream culture, seen in films such as *Boys Don't Cry* (1999), an Oscar-winning dramatization of the life of Brandon Teena, a young transgender man who was brutally murdered in a small rural town in Nebraska. For Halberstam, *Boys Don't Cry* precariously fosters a transgender gaze, adopting the subversive gaze of transman Brandon Teena, which 'reveals the ideological content of the male and female gazes', permitting the audience to explore 'both the male/female and the hetero/homo binary in narrative cinema' (2005a, p. 294). Ultimately, the transgender gaze is eschewed towards the end of the film when Brandon and his female lover Lana are portrayed as lesbians: 'the double vision of the transgender subject gives way to the universal vision of humanism; the transgender man and his lover become lesbians, and the murder seems to be simply the outcome of a vicious homophobic rage' (2005a, p. 91). Searching elsewhere, in art house films like *By Hook or By Crook* and the art of Del LaGrace Volcano, Jenny Saville and Eva Hesse and others, Halberstam reveals the possibilities for masculinities to reside in trans* bodies that do not capitulate to gender binaries. In summary, Halberstam's writing on female masculinity and trans* bodies and genders trains us toward the disjuncture between masculinity and men, opening up a wider canvass for exploring how women and trans* people perform and embody masculinities in a variety of contexts.

Failure as queer negativity

Before outlining Halberstam's thesis on failure, it is important to acknowledge that the concept of failure has been close to the heart of some queer theorists (Edelman, 2004; Love, 2007; Muñoz, 2009). After all, Muñoz (2009) astutely remarks, queers routinely fail to meet normative standards of gender and sexuality. Indeed, there is rich and diverse history of queer failure in that regard, one that is characterized by pride, celebration and defiance but also tinged with sadness, pain and death. Failure to meet gender and sexual norms has material and personal consequences that must not be ignored. Recognizing this, Muñoz treats queer failure as a mode of politics, one which is about 'doing something else' (2009, p. 154), typically anti-normative, to propel us beyond the punishing effects of gender and sexual norms. This notion of queer failure has furnished Halberstam (2011) with a platform for developing current thinking on queer negativity.

Although sympathetic to Muñoz's (2009) reading of failure and also Edelman's (2004) concept of queerness being a form of negativity that rejects the future (for an overview see Rumens, 2018), Halberstam (2011) projects a different vision of the epistemological and ethical potential of negativity. Queer negativity is conceived by Halberstam, in part, as a way of recuperating the political edginess of queerness in concepts that have negative connotations within 'heteronormative common sense', like 'failure', which lead us to 'nonconformity, anticapitalist practices, nonreproductive life styles' (2011, p. 89). Viewed in this way, Halberstam urges us to embrace the 'incoherent, the lonely, the defeated' and the melancholic formations of selfhood that queer negativity sets in motion (2011, p. 148). In so doing, Halberstam articulates visions of failure grounded in 'low theory' and popular culture (e.g. children's animated films, queer artists, punk and avantgarde performance, all of which run the risk of not being taken seriously, yet harbour potential for thinking about 'ways of knowing and being that stand outside of conventional understandings of success') (2011, p. 2). One of Halberstam's main contentions is that a queer perspective on failure can 'dismantle the logics of success and failure with which we currently live' (2011, p. 2). Success, Halberstam points out, is tightly bound to 'specific forms of reproductive maturity combined with wealth accumulation' (2011, p. 2). More precisely, Halberstam (2011) uses a particular permutation of queer negativity to problematize the reading of failure as a bad attitude on the part of the individual (e.g. the inability to accumulate wealth) rather than structural conditions (e.g. those who perpetrated the global financial crisis), and instead focus on the benefits of failure.

Read queerly, failure is said to pose a challenge to heteronormative and capitalist notions of success predicated on advancement, lineage and wealth accumulation. Like Muñoz, Halberstam's thesis places queers in the vanguard of failure: 'failing is something queers do and have always done exceptionally well; for queers failure can be a style, to cite Quentin Crisp, or a way of life, to cite Foucault' (2011, p. 3). While the consequences of violating gender and sexual binaries can be dire, even life threatening, they can also be rewarding, in that queers can rupture normative meanings of sexualities and genders. In this vein, the concept of failing as a form of queer negativity comes into its own. It can, Halberstam holds, encourage us to question established tried and tested paths of knowledge that uphold normative regimes, enabling us to generate 'visionary insights or [take] flights of fancy' (2011, p. 6). In other words, queer failure exposes 'the limits of certain forms of knowing and certain ways of inhabiting structures of knowing' (2011, pp. 11–12). This is a compelling argument that berates the disciplinary correctness that reinforces what is already known, and, for example, the 'punishing norms' that govern normative standards of gendered behaviour and relating, squelching the possibilities for alternative epistemologies and ways of relating to emerge. While Halberstam champions queer failures, not all forms of failure are queer. For example, Halberstam critiques the film *Trainspotting*, adapted from Irvine Welch's novel of the same title, for its failure to connect queerness and failure. Instead, the film (and book) links the figure of the failed, excluded white male with a 'rage that promises and delivers punishments for women and people of color' (2011, p. 92).

Halberstam excavates queer failure from a sprawling archive that includes a hodgepodge of children's animated films, punk bands, Yoko Ono and other queer artists, novels and the dark history of the Nazi regime. The methodology adopted by Halberstam to explore failure as a queer art is text-centred, illustrated vividly by readings of animated films that bring to life the potential of queering failure to imagine existing non-normative alternatives. For example, in a queer reading of Disney Pixar's animated feature film *Finding Nemo* (2011), Halberstam routes our attention to a friendship between Marlin, a paternalistic clownfish in search of his lost son, and a seemingly (un)helpful blue fish named Dory. Dory and Marlin strike up a 'queer friendship' in that it yields possibilities for the reinvention of intimacy, kinship, identity and cooperation. Dory suffers from short-term memory loss, a condition that means Dory exists in a perpetual state of forgetting wherein memories and context are experienced as fragments and flashes. Indeed, much of the humour and sentiment in the film derives from this. Halberstam observes: 'Dory represents a different, a queer and fluid form of knowing, that operates independently of coherence or linear narrative or progression' (2011, p. 54). While Marlin is initially frustrated and angered by Dory's short-term memory loss, especially because it impedes a logical progression by which he might recover his lost son, a close friendship develops through which Dory offers alternative ways of understanding and being in relation to living, dying, truth and time. It is through amnesia that Dory offers Marlin and the film's spectators a 'model of cooperation which is not dependent on payment or remunerative alliance' (2011, p. 81). Dory willingly assists Marlin in rescuing his son without expecting anything in return and is open to friendship with other ocean animals including those who might predate her. What is more, Dory's episodic memory loss facilitates her to help Marlin without knowing the nature of the bond between Marlin and Nemo, enabling Dory to relate to both fish in a friendship that prevents her from being understood within heteronormative discourses as either a stand in mother for Nemo or a new wife for Marlin. This reading of *Finding Nemo* as an instance of failure and forgetting queered, draws us toward an alternative horizon of non-normative forms of relation and action that transcend heteronormativity.

Gaga feminism

One significant development in Halberstam's thinking on gender politics is the idea of 'gaga feminism'. This concept, elaborated in *Gaga Feminism*, emerges from Halberstam's observation about the polysemic quality of the term 'gaga', conspicuously appropriated by American pop singer Lady Gaga, born under the name Stefani Germanotta. *Gaga Feminism* is not a text about Lady Gaga per se, who flits in and out of the book's analytical purview. Rather, Lady Gaga is a 'symbol for a new kind of feminism' (2012a, p. xii). For Halberstam, Gaga feminism is a

> feminism of the phony, the unreal, and the speculative, is simultaneously a monstrous outgrowth of the unstable category of 'woman' in feminist theory, a celebration of the joining of femininity to artifice, and a refusal of the mushy sentimentalism that has been siphoned into the category of womanhood.
>
> (2012a, pp. xii–xiii)

Halberstam is quick to hold at bay criticism that gaga feminism ties feminism to one person or a specific set of gender theatrics. Gaga feminism is a feminism that hints at 'emerging formulations of a gender politics for a new generation' (2012a, p. xiii) that revels in 'unbecoming women in every sense' (p. xiv) by undoing the category of woman so it is susceptible to alteration. The embodiment of gender performed by Lady Gaga is used by Halberstam to illustrate vividly gaga feminism's emphasis on experimenting with embodying gender, and how it gestures toward, not prescribes, new ways of living gender in the future. Of course, Lady Gaga is not gaga feminism personified completely and perfectly; for example, Halberstam notes the 'weird sci-fi shit' espoused in the video for one of Gaga's biggest hit records *Born This Way* (2012a, p. 132). Notably, the same song is criticized for its essentialist overtones in celebrating the self-empowerment of lesbian, gay, bisexual and transgender (LGBT) people. The song intones that they are literally *born this way*. Halberstam directs us elsewhere to songs like 'Telephone', an infectious anthemic duet with Beyoncé, which is a no-holds-barred romp in man-hating and murder that reaffirms the power of women and female friendship.

Lady Gaga's songs aside, the concept of gaga feminism channels previous themes in Halberstam's oeuvre, in particular the theme of the anarchy of childishness that was a linchpin in *The Queer Art of Failure*. Halberstam confesses that the attractiveness of gaga is because it is a 'child word' that denotes 'nonsense, madness (going gaga), surrealism (Dada), the avantgarde, pop . . . it means foolish or naïve enthusiasm, going crazy, being dotty' (2012a, p. xxv). Halberstam contends that gaga holds promise for a type of feminist politics that 'masquerades as naïve nonsense but that actually participates in big and meaningful forms of critique' (2012a, p. xxv). Gaga feminism, it is reasoned, has teeth that can cut the heteronormative fabric of society at a time when the concept of 'normal' is being beaten to a pulp by feminist and queer theorists alike. For Halberstam, the concept of gaga has something to offer feminism that enables it to disrupt, destabilize and rupture normative standards of embodying and living gender in everyday life. Gaga feminism is, if you like, the evil twin sister to neoliberal feminism that promotes a gender politics based on activities and strategies of stability and assimilation. Indeed, invocations of neoliberal feminism, most notably expressed in Sheryl Sandberg's infamous book *Lean In* (2013), are castigated by Halberstam in how it promotes individualism as an answer to the ills of structural gender inequality (see www.jackhalberstam.com/tag/sheryl-sandberg/). Neoliberal feminism is admonished by Halberstam for reproducing an unimaginative gender politics that prefers to make peace with neoliberal politics and its heteronormativity.

In stark contrast, *Gaga Feminism* is the rambunctious handbook that articulates the radical political ambition that neoliberal feminism eschews. Halberstam asserts, 'putting women in positions of power is not what gaga feminism wants' (2012a, p. 132). Gaga feminism has no interest in reaffirming 'some neoliberal concept of difference and uniqueness' (2012a, p. 141). What exactly gaga feminism wants is not fully elaborated by Halberstam who comments 'it cannot be easily summarised' (2012a, p. 133). Such an assertion chimes in with a queer politics that shuns prescribing what non-normative alternatives should be. Similarly, gaga feminism leaves a door open to a vista of possibilities that are as yet unforeseen. What gaga feminism appears to gesture toward is an 'anarchist project of cultural riot and reciprocation' (2012a, p. 137). Gaga feminism values insurrection, getting into the eye of the storm, cherishing cooperation not competition. Importantly, it rails against neoliberal individualism and instead promises to speak to the 'failures, the losers, those for whom the price of success is too high' (2012a, p. 147). In one sense, Halberstam attempts to speak to a new generation of people who are aware that we exist in cultures of 'greed' (2012a, p. 148) and who see 'multiple genders, finding male/female dichotomies to be outdated and illogical' (2012a, p. 26).

In summary, *Gaga Feminism* can be read as representing a culminating point in the development of Halberstam's ideas on gender and politics. It embraces a notion of gender fluidity espoused in *Female Masculinity* but rearticulates it to a 'new' generation of people who question the desirability of the gender binary and 'permanent' relations of intimacy (e.g. marriage). Gaga feminism converses with a generation of people who are more committed to flexibility in how gender and sexuality is lived and embodied, and who find meaning in the types of desire that emanate from non-normative alignments between gender, sex and sexuality.

The reach of Halberstam's scholarship in MOS

Discussed earlier, Halberstam's writing has made a limited but nonetheless potentially important impact on gender scholarship within MOS. The take up of Halberstam's ideas on, for example, female masculinity and queer failure within the MOS field has, in part, been conditioned by the introduction of poststructuralist feminist and queer theories into the same domain. Queer theory first made an impression in MOS with the publication of an essay in 1996 by feminist political theorists J.K. Gibson-Graham on how queer theory might be able to inspire alternative, non-normative modes of organizing beyond capitalism. Notably, Halberstam voices admiration for Gibson-Graham's work on this topic, enlisting it as an illustration of 'gaga politics' that can crystallize from gaga feminism (2012a, p. 126). Still, it was almost another five years before Martin Parker (2001; 2002) set a different tone for queer theorizing by drawing on the work of Judith Butler and Eve Kosofsky Sedgwick to theorize management as performative. As queer theory scholarship within MOS has grown in scope, so more MOS scholars have unlocked doors to queer theorizing that do not lead to Butler, Sedgwick and Foucault, the holy trinity of queer theorists, to whom all queer theory roads appear to guide us (for an overview see Rumens, 2018). Within this strand of literature, Halberstam's ideas have been put to service in research on trans* gender identities and bodies in the workplace (Muhr and Sullivan, 2013; Muhr, Sullivan, and Rich, 2016; Schilt and Westbrook, 2009). Elsewhere, Halberstam's work (e.g. on female masculinity) has been utilized by MOS scholars working within a poststructuralist feminist vein (Pullen and Vachhani, 2018) and gender studies researchers who have explored women's performance of masculinity within male dominated work contexts (Denissen and Saguy, 2014). Emergent work on queer failure and queering heterosexuality in organizational settings has also signalled the promise of Halberstam's writing as a conceptual resource for MOS scholars (Rumens, 2018).

Illustrating the potential of Halberstam's research on trans* bodies and lives, Muhr, Sullivan, and Rich (2016) embrace Halberstam's (1998; 2005a) assertion that we must display greater sensitivity to gender variance and trans* gender mobilities, since the embodied experiences of living a trans* gender will vary amongst those who identify as transsexual, genderqueer, non-binary, drag kings and queens, and so on. Likewise, Muhr, Sullivan, and Rich (2016) maintain that the exploration of gender variance and transgression must be situated within a material analysis of trans* people's everyday lives. Illustrating this empirically, Muhr, Sullivan, and Rich (2016) examine the work experiences of Claire, a MtF transwoman, and develop the concept of 'situated transgressiveness' to denote how the 'potential for transgressiveness within work and professional contexts is heavily nuanced, fluid and contingent on a variety of situated work contexts, such as roles, locales and interactions with others' (2016, p. 66). For example, Muhr, Sullivan, and Rich (2016, p. 65) note how Claire makes no attempt to 'mask or downplay her trans body, regardless of audience resistance', when working in a public advocacy role for transgender rights. In these situations, Claire advocates and embodies gender fluidity. In her managerial role, Claire manages her trans identity according to the various requirements made of her by work colleagues. In these instances, gender binaries can be preserved through gender performances that are tailored to situational demands which may entail downplaying gender, and foregrounding the 'gender neutral' characteristics associated with being 'professional'. Claire's transgression of the gender binary is influenced by normative expectations of sex, gender, work and professionalism, all of which intermingle in different ways to enable and constrain how Claire can live her work career and life as a transwoman.

Somewhat similarly, Pullen and Vachhani elegantly deploy Halberstam's (1998) notion of female masculinity to 'read feminine leadership subversively' to trouble the binary division between masculinity and femininity (2018, p. 127). Feminine leadership circulates as a set of discourses that variously link women to leadership within the confines of gender stereotypes. For instance, feminine leadership discourse promulgates participatory and non-hierarchical practices that are more easily performed by women not men, while other permutations of feminine leadership discourse suggest such practices can bring a softer quality to the workplace through femininities that are coded in terms of cooperation, nurturing and empathy. Pullen and Vachhani (2018) turn to Halberstam's notion of female masculinity to problematize feminine leadership discourse by showing how, for example, it reproduces gender stereotypes that sustain a masculine/feminine binary. More precisely, feminine leadership is exposed as a contradictory site, wherein if women do not perform normative femininity well enough, they are failures; equally, if they do not 'demonstrate masculine leadership through careful mimesis, they have failed' (2018, p. 135). They argue: 'female masculinity is other to not only the masculine but the feminine, and this disrupts simplistic and oppressive dualistic conceptions of gender reproduced in analyses of the effectiveness of feminine leadership' (2018, p. 136). Tapping into Halberstam's queer-feminist politics of disruption, Pullen and Vachhani (2018) challenge how feminine leadership discourse presupposes essential gender differences between women and men, thus opening up opportunities for thinking through a feminist ethics of sexual difference that is based on a notion of relationality, directing attention to how leadership is practiced between gendered subjects, 'where ethics are the relationships between those subjects' (2018, p. 143).

Elsewhere, Rumens (2018) underscores the value of Halberstam's notion of queer failure for studying LGBT sexualities and genders in the workplace. Rumens articulates this twofold. First, the empirical examination of how LGBT people fail to meet organizational norms relating to sexuality and gender and the reparative strategies some adopt to avoid such failure constitutes an important, but still understudied, focal point in MOS scholarship. Suggesting that MOS scholars carry out empirical research on this type of failure (e.g. the failure of 'queers') and the myriad forms it can take in the workplace, insights are potentially opened up for understanding how the performance of failure can enable LGBT subjects to move toward queer(er) ways of un/becoming and organizing at work. After all, Halberstam (2011) asserts that failure is happening all around us, and some of those failures may have a queer bent that can provide insights into existing non-normative alternative ways of living sexuality and gender at work. Second, there is the failure experienced in pursuing this kind of research, which in some business and management schools is read negatively as the failure to meet the normative standards of what is 'worthy' and 'credible' MOS scholarship. Such invocations of failure and success can reveal the toxicity of the here and now. For Rumens, instances where MOS researchers are dissuaded from researching organization LGBT sexualities (see Ozturk and Rumens, 2014), business and management schools are, in one sense, telling us there is no future for LGBT people. By complying with such normative injunctions, we might find ourselves complicit in writing the future out of the organizational lives of LGBT subjects. Queer failure, then, is one means by which we can disrupt the heteronormativity of business and management schools, and reimagine queer(er) organizational futures. Following Halberstam's (2011) exhortation about looking for existing queer failures, MOS researchers could turn to those LGBT subjects who are 'experts' (but not the only experts) at failing, providing insights into non-normative alternatives for living and relating as gendered and sexual subjects at work.

Conclusion

This chapter has outlined J. Jack Halberstam's contribution to cultural studies, in particular to a queer-feminist politics of disruption that aims to seek out existing non-normative forms of living gender and sexuality. While Halberstam's research is mostly confined to textual analyses of novels, songs, films, visual art and performance, the ideas developed within Halberstam's wide canon of literature hold enormous value for MOS researchers. Concepts including female masculinity and queer failure have been mobilized by MOS scholars to advance research on the dynamics between gender, fluidity and embodiment. They can enable us to explore the contextual contingencies of transgressing the gender binary at work and invite us to rupture feminine leadership discourse that reproduces the gender binary. Yet there is still scope for MOS scholars to delve into Halberstam's archive more broadly and deeply to explore gender, fluidity and embodiment in organizations. We might engineer a new organization feminist politics that is based on the 'gaga' concept, whereby MOS scholars examine how gendered subjects are re-imagining the organizational worlds they occupy and their sense of a meaningful future. This chapter has shown how Halberstam's ideas can function as potent conceptual resources for destabilizing and reshaping the gendered contours of the MOS field we currently inhabit.

Recommended reading

Original text by Halberstam

Halberstam, J. (1998). *Female masculinity*. Durham: Duke University Press.

Key academic text

Gardiner, J. K. (2012). Female masculinity and phallic women – Unruly concepts. *Feminist Studies*, 38(3), pp. 597–624.

Accessible resource

https://bullybloggers.wordpress.com/about/ is the website for Bully Bloggers, a queer word art group, which contains blogs and resources written by Halberstam.

References

Butler, J. (1990). *Gender trouble: Feminism and the subversion of identity*. New York, NY: Routledge.
Butler, J. (1993). *Bodies that matter: On the limits of sex*. London: Routledge.

Butler, J. (2004). *Undoing gender*. New York, NY: Routledge.

Denissen, A. M. and Saguy, A. C. (2014). Gendered homophobia and the contradictions of workplace discrimination for women in the building trades. *Gender & Society*, 28(3), 381–403.

Edelman, L. (2004). *No future: Queer theory and the death drive*. Durham: Duke University Press.

Gibson-Graham, J. K. (1996). Queer(y)ing capitalist organization. *Organization*, 3(4), pp. 541–545.

Halberstam, J. (1991). Skinflick: Posthuman gender in Jonathan Demme's *The silence of the lambs*. *Camera Obscura*, 9(3), pp. 36–53.

Halberstam, J. (1993). Technologies of monstrosity: Bram Stoker's *Dracula*. *Victorian Studies*, 36(3), pp. 333–352.

Halberstam, J. (1995). *Skin shows: Gothic horror and the technology of monsters*. Durham: Duke University Press.

Halberstam, J. (1997). Mackdaddy, superfly, rapper: Gender, race, and masculinity in the drag king scene. *Social Text*, (52/53), pp. 105–131.

Halberstam, J. (1998). *Female masculinity*. Durham: Duke University Press.

Halberstam, J. (2001). Oh behave! Austin powers and the drag kings. *GLQ: A Journal of Lesbian and Gay Studies*, 7(3), pp. 425–452.

Halberstam, J. (2003a). What's that smell? Queer temporalities and subcultural lives. *International Journal of Cultural Studies*, 6(3), pp. 313–333.

Halberstam, J. (2003b). Reflections on queer studies and queer pedagogy. *Journal of Homosexuality*, 45(2–4), pp. 361–364.

Halberstam, J. (2005a). *In a queer time and place: Transgender bodies, subcultural lives*. New York, NY: New York University Press.

Halberstam, J. (2005b). Shame and white gay masculinity. *Social Text*, 23(3–4, 84–85), pp. 219–233.

Halberstam, J. (2008). The anti-social turn in queer studies. *Graduate Journal of Social Science*, 5(2), pp. 140–156.

Halberstam, J. (2011). *The queer art of failure*. Durham: Duke University Press.

Halberstam, J. (2012a). *Gaga feminism: Sex, gender, and the end of normal*. Boston: Beacon Press.

Halberstam, J. (2012b). Global female masculinities. *Sexualities*, 15(3–4), pp. 336–354.

Halberstam, J. (2013). Go gaga: Anarchy, chaos, and the wild. *Social Text*, 31(3, 116), pp. 123–134.

Halberstam, J. (2018). *Trans* A quick and quirky account of gender variability*. Oakland: University of California Press.

Love, H. (2007). Compulsory happiness and queer existence. *New Formations*, 63, pp. 52–65.

Muhr, S. L. and Sullivan, K. R. (2013). 'None so queer as folk': Gendered expectations and transgressive bodies in leadership. *Leadership*, 9(3), pp. 416–435.

Muhr, S. L., Sullivan, K. R. and Rich, C. (2016). Situated transgressiveness: Exploring one transwoman's lived experiences across three situated contexts. *Gender, Work & Organization*, 23(1), pp. 52–70.

Muñoz, J. E. (2009). *Cruising utopia: The then and there of queer futurity*. New York, NY: New York University Press.

Ozturk, M. B. and Rumens, N. (2014). Gay male academics in UK business and management schools: Negotiating heteronormativities in everyday work life. *British Journal of Management*, 25(3), pp. 503–517.

Parker, M. (2001). Fucking management: Queer, theory and reflexivity. *Ephemera*, 1(1), pp. 36–53.

Parker, M. (2002). Queering management and organization. *Gender, Work & Organization*, 9(2), pp. 146–166.

Pullen, A. and Vachhani, S. J. (2018). Examining the politics of gendered difference in feminine leadership: The absence of 'Female Masculinity'. In: A. Sujana, and A. Sheridan, eds., *Inclusive leadership*. Basingstoke: Palgrave Macmillan, pp. 125–149.

Rumens, N. (2018). *Queer business: Queering organisation sexualities*. New York, NY: Routledge.

Sandberg, S. (2013). *Lean in: Women, work, and the will to lead*. New York, NY: Random House.

Schilt, K., and Westbrook, L. (2009). Doing gender, doing heteronormativity: 'Gender Normals', transgender people, and the social maintenance of heterosexuality. *Gender & Society*, 23(4), pp. 440–464.

Volcano, D. L. and Halberstam, J. (1999). *The drag king book*. London: Serpent's Tail.

Warner, M. (1993). *Fear of a queer planet: Queer politics and social theory*. Minneapolis, MN: University of Minnesota Press.

Index

abjection 45–48, 50–52
academic activism 5, 75, 87
Acker, Joan: academic career 8–9;
    body in organizations 16; job
    evaluation systems 12; on social
    stratification 10; and van Houten
    10–11; on wage setting 11–12
Affect 82–84; affect theory (Tomkins)
    83–84

Bakhtin, Mikhail 43
Benschop, Yvonne 3
Beyoncé 100–101
body: absence of 16–17; corporealities
    of the 83; desire and 66; as locus
    of semiotic chora 43–44; as
    managerial control object 16–17;
    in organizations 16; relationship
    between text and 6; as semiotic chora
    45; women's relationship to 33;
    Wittig, Monique, Lesbian Body 71
Butler, Judith 34, 77, 102

Camus, Albert 26, 38n3
Castoriadis, Cornelius 55
childishness, anarchy of 101
class: class inequalities 20; class
    stratification, sex vs. class 10; see
    also gender and class
critical management studies (CMS)
    78, 79

de Beauvoir, Simone: Adieux 27; on
    being a woman 28; biography of
    26–27; The Coming of Age 30; on
    embodiment 32–33; The Ethics
    of Ambiguity 29–30; impact of

4; influences of 26–27; influence
    within organization studies 34–36;
    on inter-subjectivity 27–28; Les
    Temps Modernes 27; The Second Sex
    27–29, 32–34; She Came to Stay
    27; on status of the Other 28–29; on
    strategies for women 32; on women's
    otherness 35; writings of 25, 27
Deleuze, Gilles 59
Derrida, Jacques 77
de Staël, Madame 63
d'Estaing, Giscard 61
disembodiment 83; disembodied
    worker 16
Douglas, Mary 46

embodiment 32–33, 44, 96–97; diverse
    embodiments 96; see also body;
    disembodiment
Epistemology of the Closet (Sedgwick)
    78; closet, the, discursive structure
    of 67
Equality Act of 2010 (UK) 37
Erasmus prize 71n3
Ethics of Ambiguity, The (de Beauvoir)
    29–30

failure, queer perspective on 97–100
Fawcett Society 37
female masculinities 67–68,
    92, 95–97, 102–104; Female
    Masculinity (Halberstam) 95; drag
    kings 96
feminine leadership 103–104
femininity: entrapment as sign of 31;
    inferior status to 35; Otherness and
    30; as state of serfdom 31–32

feminism: feminist scholarship 9; feminist theories 13–18; neoliberal 101; religion vs. 49; Sedgwick on 87; patriarchy 47; second-wave feminist theory 29
Finding Nemo (film) 99–100
forbidden love 63–68
foreignness 52–53; *see also* Otherness/ the Other; uncanny strangeness
Foucault, Michel 69
French Academy 60–63
Freud, Sigmund 52–53; Freudian law of castration 49
'fucking management,' as act of deconstruction 78–79

gaga feminism 92, 100–102
gender: as constitutive part of social structures 15; as perpetual process of 'un/doing' 34–35
gender ambiguous 93–94; gender divisions 14; gender binary 103; gender embodiment 96; gender fluidity 94, 96, 102, 103; gendered leadership 68; gendered self 31; gendered substructure 15–16, 17–18; living gender 6, 100–101, 105
gender and class: hierarchies 12, 36; inequalities 13
gendered organizations: definition of 14; feminist theory of 13–18; identities in 15; *see also* gender; organizations
Gender, Work, and Organization (Sedgwick) 78
Gibson-Graham, J.K. 102

Halberstam, J. Jack 6–7; biography of 93–95; Bully Bloggers 93; female masculinities and 95–97; *Female Masculinity* 95; gaga feminism 100–102; *Gaga Feminism* 100–102; as gender ambiguous 93–94; *In a Queer Time and Place* 97; on masculinities residing in trans* bodies 97; *The Queer Art of Failure* 101; on queer negativity 97–100; queer theory and 95; research interests 93; *Trans* 94; trans* studies and 92
happy objects, as delusive 81–82
Hawthorne studies 2, 3, 10

Hegel, Georg 26–27
Hekanaho, Pia 67–68
hermeneutics of recovery of meaning 86; hermeneutics of suspicion 86
heteronormativity 92–93; heteronormative matrix of representation 78; heterosexual/ homosexual binary 92–93
HIV/AIDS activism 78, 87
homosexuality 63–64, 67–68

ideal worker: characteristics of 16–17; description of 2
In a Queer Time and Place (Halberstam) 97
indigenous peoples, as doubly Othered 35
inequalities: class 20; definition of 19; legitimacy of 20; visibility of 19–20
inequality regimes: challenging 20; changing 20; components of 19; definition of 18; intersectional 19; key publications 18
intersectionality, in inequality regimes 18–20; intersectional inequalities 19, 20
intersubjectivity 27–28, 54, 56

Klein, Melanie 85
Kristeva, Julia 4–5; awards earned 42; biography of 42–43; on feminism 48–49; feminism vs. religion 49; inspiring feminist thinking 48; linking motherhood, religion and death 53–54; on maternal body 47; *Powers of Horror* 45; on semanalysis 43; on signification process 43; *Strangers to Ourselves* 52; on subject as flesh in language 45; symbolic and theorizing on subjectivity 44; 'Woman's Time' 49

Lacan, Jacques 45; Lacanian symbolic 47, 49, 55; Lacanian Law of the Father 49
Lady Gaga (Stefani Germanotta) 100–101
leadership: ethical 69; feminine 103–104; gendered understanding of 68
Lévi-Strauss, Claude 61
LGBT sexualities in the workplace 104

management and organization (MOS):
feminist influence on 13; Halberstam
and 92; queer failure in 102; queer
theory scholarship in 102
Masculinity 2, 12, 15, 36, 67, 93–97,
102–105; engineered masculinity
96; misogyny 48
materialist feminist sociology 12–13
motherhood 47; maternal, as pre-
lingual 48; maternal authority
46–47; matricide 46
Merleau Ponty, Maurice 26, 32
Memoirs of Hadrian (Yourcenar) 60,
68–71
men: semiotic chora and 43–44;
sexualization of the body 17
#MeToo social media campaign 87

occupational segregation by sex 10–11
organizations: abjection of the
body in 50–52; the body in 16;
as consequence of performative
acts 80; exploiting desire for
recognition 36; feminist theory of
gender in 13; as gender-neutral 11;
impact of sex 10; organizational
inequity 35; organizational life,
open secrets of 67; organizational
logic 14–16; queer approaches to
60; sex structuring in 10–11; work
environment 16, 51, 104; *see also*
gendered organizations
organization studies: de Beauvoir and
34–36; feminist approaches to 11;
silences in 59
organization theory 75, 77–78, 83
Otherness/the Other: de Beauvoir
and 28–29, 35; femininity equated
to 30; of indigenous peoples 35;
objectification 30; oppressive
condition of 47; strangeness and
54–55; transcending 36; woman as
socially constructed as 35

*Paranoid Reading and Reparative
Reading* (Sedgwick) 85; paranoid
reading 86
performativity: explicit 81;
management as 102; of women

business owners 35; *see also* queer
performativities
periperformative spatialities 80–81
Powers of Horror (Kristeva) 45
PricewaterhouseCoopers (PwC) 26,
36–37
productive shame 83–84
psychoanalytic theory 52, 54–55
pursuit of happiness 81–82

Queer Art of Failure, The (Halberstam)
101
queer failure 92, 97–100, 104
queering management 78–79; queer
negativity 6–7, 97–100
queer performativities 75–78, 82–83,
87–88; *see also* performativity
queer theory 60, 78, 95, 102; queer
witness 77–82; queer survival 76

reparative readings 85, 86–87
Rose, Jacqueline 54
Royal Belgian Academy 71n3

same-sex relationships 63–64;
same-sex attraction 70
Sartre, Jean-Paul 26, 38n3
Second Sex, The (de Beauvoir):
criticisms of 32–34; description of
27–29; as racist 33; Sartre writing
38n3
Sedgwick, Eve Kosofsky 5–6; as
academic activist 87; on affect
as free radical 83; on charged
pairings 67; corporealities of
writing and lived experience
76–77; *Epistemology of the
Closet* 78; on epistemology of
the closet 67; *Gender, Work, and
Organization* 78; influencing
feminism 87; overlooked
pedagogical work 86; on paranoid
reading 86; *Paranoid Reading and
Reparative Reading* 85; Patton
and 85; on periperformatives 80;
queer performativity (*see* queer
performativities); queer theory and
75; *Tendencies* 79
self-reflexivity 5, 54, 68

semiotic chora 43–45; semiotic
motility 50
sex inequality, sex segregation, job
evaluation 10–12
sexuality: absence of 17; as managerial
control object 16–17; as prison of
desiring 66
She Came to Stay (de Beauvoir) 27;
dress codes, sexualized 37; sexual
fluidity 60
silences: in *Alexis* 64–65; of inhibitions
and taboos 65; in literary texts 59; in
organization studies 59
situated transgressiveness 103
social construction 2–3, 11, 29, 34–35
socialization, sex differences in 10–11;
social stratification 10
spatial organization 79–80
speech-act theory 79
strangeness of our unconscious
54–55, 56
Strangers to Ourselves (Kristeva) 52
subjectivity, Kristeva's theorization
on 44
symbolic 43, 47, 53–55; symbolic
language 45–46; symbolic order 44,
47–51

Tendencies (Sedgwick) 79
Todorov, Tzvetan 43

trans* studies 94–95; trans* bodies
97, 103; *Trans* (Halberstam) 94;
transgender gaze 97

uncanny strangeness 52–53; *see also*
foreignness

waged labour 11; wage gap 11–12
women: accepting their entrapment 31;
butch 96; conforming to feminine
role 31; embracing male rationality
33; feminine leadership 103–104;
in management 13; as other 2–3;
political transformation through
social reorganization 32; relationship
to their bodies 33; relegated to
secondary status 28; semiotic chora
and 43–44; sexualization of the
body 17; asocially constructed as
the Other 35; striving to become
intellectuals 32; supporting
themselves financially 32

Yourcenar, Marguerite 5; *Alexis* 63–68;
biography of 61–62; elected to French
Academy 60–63; Erasmus prize
71n3; Frick and 61; Galey and 61;
Le coup de grâce 61; literary work of
59; *Memoirs of Hadrian* 60, 68–71;
Wilson and 61; Woolf and 71n2

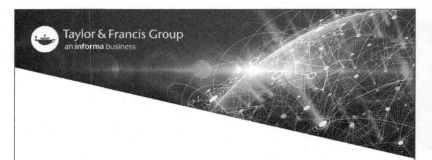

Printed in the United States
by Baker & Taylor Publisher Services